writing and seeing architecture

University of Minnesota Press Minneapolis – London

writing and seeing architecture

Christian de **Portzamparc** and Philippe **Sollers**

translated by Catherine Tihanyi **foreword by** Deborah Hauptmann

This book was published with the support of the French Ministry of Culture—National Book Center. Cet ouvrage a été publié avec l'assistance du Ministère chargé de la culture—Centre National du Livre.

Originally published in French as *Voir écrire,* by Christian de Portzamparc and Philippe Sollers. Copyright 2003 by Callmann-Lévy.

English translation copyright 2008 by the Regents of the University of Minnesota

Foreword copyright 2008 by the Regents of the University of Minnesota

All rights reserved. No part of this publication may be reproduced, stored in a retrieval system, or transmitted, in any form or by any means, electronic, mechanical, photocopying, recording, or otherwise, without the prior written permission of the publisher.

Published by the University of Minnesota Press
111 Third Avenue South, Suite 290
Minneapolis, MN 55401-2520
http://www.upress.umn.edu

Library of Congress Cataloging-in-Publication Data

Portzamparc, Christian de, 1944–
    [Voir Écrire]
    Writing and seeing architecture / Christian de Portzamparc and Philippe Sollers ; translated by Catherine Tihanyi ; foreword by Deborah Hauptmann.
        p.   cm.
    Includes bibliographical references.
    ISBN 978-0-8166-4567-1 (hc : alk. paper) — ISBN 978-0-8166-4568-8 (pb : alk. paper)
    1. Architecture and society.   2. Architecture, Modern—20th century—Philosophy.   3. Literature and society.   I. Sollers, Philippe, 1936–   II. Title.
    NX180.S6P6713 2008
    730.1—dc22

                                                                        2007048155

Printed in the United States of America on acid-free paper

The University of Minnesota is an equal-opportunity educator and employer.

16 15 14 13 12 11 10 09 08   10 9 8 7 6 5 4 3 2 1

Contents

Foreword

Deborah Hauptmann

Let us begin at the consciousness of speaking, at this reciprocal contamination of the words and the means, where that which writes must first see *(voir écrire)*.

If we inquire into the history of literature and of architecture over the past forty years, we are struck by the complexity and the ambiguity of the adventure, qualities most evident in the fact that new spaces and new means of writing and drawing—of making—were invented, ones that profoundly modified our understanding of both communication and the image, of both space and time, ones that were combined with a reflexivity within certain texts and certain buildings that rendered them somehow indefinitely open in and of themselves and in which there appeared something radically other and, more important, something that would be linked to an increasingly urgent meditation on writing, exemplified, perhaps most succinctly, in what Derrida called "grammatology." The turning point of this era, the *end* of philosophy and *beginning* of theory, came to be known simply as 1968. It was a time in which we watched Philippe Sollers tracing the rupture in writing to the inside-out of textual space expressed in the multiple singularities of, among others, Lautréamont/Mallarmé and Artaud/

Bataille. We saw Christian de Portzamparc dream his tower at Marne-la-Vallée, a tower of water and green evincing the distanced proximity between the utilitarian and the symbolic. And simultaneously the architect-poet John Hejduk brought us to the Wall House, to movement itself, to passage between the earth, sea, and sky. We include Hejduk here as a moment of exception, as a having been that persists; we offer his name as a sleeper. Some*one* who "sleeps beyond the spectacle, so as to find again time lost, things past" (chapter 8).

In *Writing and Seeing Architecture* we encounter a call to thinking—if thinking can be grasped as a bursting and an overflow that speaks, a grasping that does not fix thought within a mode of thinking that the very appearance of this writer, this architect, has served to transform and deny. Where some have seen a failure and an end, something exhausted, precious, they sense a recommencement, a call toward the once believed yet unachieved risk: speaking of form, of poetry, of the necessary and transformative link between poetry and society. Not the word, as such, but the affirmation of wor(l)d in a new form of writing; not the object, as such, but the radical astonishment we must retain when faced with the presence of very small, very modest, and intimate things. Today, such a position designates both a past and a future, or rather this point in time where the past–future distinction dissolves, where the past seems accessible from every direction and the future appears to flow back toward us from that turning point, that which once represented itself as the end of philosophy, the moment of theory, that once beginning of the turn whose unforeseeable effects we have not begun to decipher. As if a limit had been crossed, we are confronted with a great interval, a duration *(durée)* of consistency running forty years and then another century further, an unfolding that took place against the philosophical and aesthetic background of Marx, Nietzsche, Heidegger, and Freud; of Manet and Cézanne, Mallarmé and Rimbaud, Wagner and Debussy, Le Corbusier and Wright—a background itself referring to an unprecedented scientific, economic, and technical mutation. Ungraspable space in the absence of time, an endless but finite totality. Another logic, another function of the perhaps still empty pronoun we have just employed: we.

Of course this "we" is that of a compound of writing extracted from, inserted between, fragments of Sollers's writing and my own. The inside-out of another's words: in time, all such debts are repaid. But for now I have stolen this moment, not like a thief but like the child pinching a coin from a favorite uncle's pocket (a coin placed there in anticipation of just such an exchange); no doubt those familiar with *Tel Quel,* and certainly Sollers, would well understand. This said, if I am lucky, this image (my fingers in the pocket of Sollers) has successfully induced a stop because it is now necessary to begin this foreword again. Of course, the problem—whether it lies in the unbelievable as with Sollers or the unlivable as with de Portzamparc—is always in knowing how to begin.

Writing and Seeing Architecture records a dialogic journey taking place between two French intellectuals, contemporaries and friends: a novelist/editor/theorist and an architect/artist/writer. Within these pages the voices of Sollers and de Portzamparc *(homo loquax)* have been captured as/if/in theoretical discourse, yet that which we hear, that which we read, is also a conversation between two makers *(homo faber).* There can be no doubt that Sollers and de Portzamparc have each in their own right invented worlds; they have constructed form through means that while differing in matter have at the same time shared greatly in substance. And here in the space opened by speech, their roles, their words, often seamlessly merge and interchange. As Sollers, referring to the exchange between painters and poets, says of Picasso that "the eye listens," so too might we not say at times in the exchange between writer and architect that the voice sees. "Language is an eye, an ear, a sense of smell," Sollers says of Claudel; and with these "organs of perception"—these senses so perfected—it might be said that both Sollers and de Portzamparc have perfected seeing to the point of making it a sense of touch. Thus, these conversations surpass the shades of meaning restricted to intelligence alone, allowing us to witness, to feel, a more accurate perception of structure and movement, of spatiotemporal relations, in all their rhythms.

The intellectual trajectory along which these dialogues take place has been sketched out above, and the terrain on which it now (tacitly, invisibly) moves will be recognizable to anyone familiar with the work of such thinkers as Michel Foucault, Jacques Derrida, Jacques Lacan, Roland Barthes, Julia Kristeva, Georges Bataille, and Friedrich Nietzsche. Moreover, the literary journal *Tel Quel* will no doubt be familiar to anyone whose interest crosses the domain of sociocultural theory in general and literary criticism, architecture, and art theory more specifically. It is arguable, in fact, that any discourse over that past forty years that has touched on semiotics as an interdisciplinary concern has crossed, in one way or the other, the thresholds of the *Tel Quel* group. For instance, in 1960s literary theory on both sides of the Atlantic, Barthes's desanctioning of the (biographically centric) author or the removal of authority from the author turned scriptor ("The Death of the Author," 1967, first published in America) and Kristeva's concept of intertextuality ("Word, Dialogue, and Novel," 1969) have impacted our thinking on linguistic phenomena and the origin (or *non*-originality) of textual content and, further, on the invention of new forms of writing. Clearly such theories transformed thinking in architecture as well; for instance, Diana Agrest and Mario Gandelsonas's work on semiotics and architecture ("Semiotics and Architecture: Ideological Consumption or Theoretical Work," 1973) was being published in the first issue of *Oppositions*. With this the influence of the French intellectual climate (not to mention the Italian discourse on semiotics) was brought to the center of Anglo-American discourse in architecture theory. De Portzamparc will say that this turn toward semiotics in architecture took a misguided path, one that seemed to provide a "stumbling block for architecture precisely because, by denying the specific character of space, by denying its autonomy from language" (chapter 3) it was unable to grasp architecture. By this he understands its "mode of existence of space and of the visible such as perceptions, sensations, light, geometry, movements" (chapter 5)—architecture, such as it is *(tel quel)*. But he will also suggest that with Kristeva's "inter-textuality" we understood that "one text responds to another," and that with this it might also be imagined that so too "space responds to space."

Yet to properly disentwine the conceptual differentiations within these complex and highly specific discourses on what would come to be called poststructural linguistics is beyond both the scope and the necessity of this foreword. Here it must be enough simply to remind the reader of the theoretically rich framework on which these conversations at once invisibly and yet palpably hang. It might well be that the intellectual history of the French-American discourse has become so well entrenched in much of our thinking that it has inadvertently fallen to the domain of what I would like to call a misplaced significance. Nevertheless, it is impossible to forget (and it would be erroneous to dismiss) one of the best known of these cross-fertilizations (at least with regard to architecture) in both theory and practice; I am referring, of course, to the copious exchanges that took place in the 1980s and 1990s between Peter Eisenman and Jacques Derrida. There was also the work of Mark Wigley, with numerous essays on Derrida and the concept of deconstruction published in the 1980s, culminating in *The Architecture of Deconstruction: Derrida's Haunt* (1995). However, while these examples can be said to follow from this intellectual history, they nevertheless took a different course from the one contained in the following pages. It is also worth taking a moment to recall the impact that Denis Hollier's writing on Bataille had on architectural discourse; this work began in French in the early 1970s, yet only later made its presence fully felt with his *Against Architecture* (English translation, 1989). In the following pages the reader will no doubt recognize the architectural modalities of Bataille's pyramid and labyrinth and the violence upon the body that these forms inscribe, rethought through the figures of the tower and the cave.

The conversation transcriptions that compose *Writing and Seeing Architecture* have been given chapter titles that indicate the disposition of the various meetings. Yet the multiple unity of the issues raised is thoroughly imbricated throughout these dialogues, and it is clearly the recurring questions—contingently (if not differentially) framed—and not the provisional answers that coalesce to produce a heterogeneous (albeit at times elliptical) discourse. These discussions take place after the moment marked by 9/11, and this turn is the point on which the first dialogue begins. Thus Sollers and de Portzamparc challenge the horizon of human reference, and throughout, in the sense of both memory and matter, questions pertaining to what can be called the horizon of experience persist. Of course, Paul Virilio also saw de Portzamparc's fascination with horizons, not with the line that finitely measures but with the line that infinitely moves and recedes, allowing the measureless to be felt. The "diminutive infinite," as Sollers will refer to it while citing Cézanne: "since sensations are the basis of my business, I believe I am impenetrable" (chapter 4). Here the question goes to the very condition of a sensorial world, to the truth of sensations, to the possibility of making the infinite appear as the transformation of our day's presence. In one way or another, the queries posed in these conversations both begin and return continuously to issues pertaining to the proximity, to the distance or the distanceless space occurring between thought and language and thus to the challenge of representation, to the relation between thought and that which cannot be brought under the determinant of structure. Here, in writing so seen, these conversations do ask not only about the quantities, the formulas, with which objects begin and inquire into the qualities formed and the states of things in which bodies are located but also, and more important, how visibilities might be extracted from objects and qualities from things and how it is that sensation comes to be in things. Thus, the image, the visible, the question of form is mediated wherein speech is spontaneous and vision is receptive (not to ever confuse the first as active and the second as passive). However, here Sollers and de Portzamparc must work between two modalities: between language and image, not only between content and form per se.

"Can we think without language?" De Portzamparc poses this question again and again. It is an architect's question, enunciating perhaps a nonproblem for Sollers, who at a still point obliquely responds: "to be at the same time in the space of the written, in the broad sense of the word, and in the image, the drawing, provokes unease"; and a few moments later he replies, again indirectly, "Thenceforth, architecture, instead of manifesting itself in the foundations, will manifest itself increasingly as an envelopment, a gap, a way of intervening into something that is already there" (chapter 7). Bringing forward without the need to look back, the already there, the having been that persists, an interval in time, perhaps, but certainly an intervening in space. And this is the term they turn to again and again—*intervention*—by which they are speaking of a slicing through *(tranchant)* that is decisive, a precise cut in which a hollowness is created so as to assemble the plurality of things. With this I. M. Pei's National Gallery in Washington is discussed over and over again, and yet, like Baudelaire's Paris, it is never actually named; it is located, it is a site in which the situation itself is given place. The intervention /as/ event. In this sense they speak of an inevitable leap forward, or perhaps a recapitulation to the importance of site, of a cohesion that can be achieved only case by case. This is also an attribute that de Portzamparc refers to his Age III of the city. "In the face of space possessed by the confining of time, itself given up to computation, an intervention, whether it be with language or with architecture, would consist of freeing what can be freed" (chapter 8). A space freed for the play of time: with Heidegger they attempt a call to a clearing of space, *alētheia*, though this too goes unnamed.

Some may see in these conversations a return to humanism, a rejection of technological determinism following Heidegger. And in the current climate of architectural practice, guided too often by technomanagerial processes, computational methods, and data-driven design—the formula and the form—Sollers and de Portzamparc do offer a renewal of both thinking and doing that reinstantiates the body (both corporeal and incorporeal) and remaps the space of poetics at the core of the body politic. It might be possible to imagine a phenomenological disposition here, but that would be a mistake. For although the conversations often revolve on comments pertaining to perception, their concerns can be said more accurately to hold to the underlying questions (which return again and again): Of what can architecture be made to speak? How is it that form can be understood to gather, to live, to breathe? Sollers and de Portzamparc are not here describing a return to things, to phenomenological appearances guided by intentionality, much less meaning. In short, they are not questioning the consciousness *of* a thing; they are positing the conditions of consciousness *as* a thing. Consciousness *is* and thus it is unnecessary to take recourse to meaning in order to discuss memory and perception, content and image, that which simultaneously conceals and reveals. Or as Sollers will say of Rimbaud's *Illuminations:* "a vision that doesn't find its beginning in the program of metaphysics, that doesn't let itself be brought back to metaphysics's fold . . . This stands as the opposite of a vision in which it is no longer possible to discern a difference between the word that reaches its destination and the vision that is already there. Architecture, in my opinion, should be practiced so as to let these Cities exist" (chapter 2).

Writing and Seeing Architecture draws forward the moments of incandescence that punctuate perception and thus situates word and image not as representation but more directly, sensorially, extensively in space, intensively in time, in experience *such as it is.* It seeks to give color to the vowels, thickening our understanding of both the limits and the liberations taking place over what Sollers and de Portzamparc refer to as singularities, not the *Singular Objects of Architecture* (by Baudrillard and Nouvel, published by the University of Minnesota Press, 2002), but the multiple singularity of poetic experience. That which, if only permitted, might burst forth with a subject force that slices through the closure of time, of space and language; an encompassing and intervening force that may still be found within the action that *is* architecture.

Acknowledgments

The authors would like to thank the Maison des Écrivains and the University of Paris VI–La Villette School of Architecture for the initiative to sponsor a conference between architects and philosophers. The project, Urban Passages, was a series of six encounters between writers and architects in 1997 and 1998 that made headlines both inside and outside the school. The extended dialogue between Christian de Portzamparc and Philippe Sollers that was part of that project forms the basis of the present text. The five other pairs of participants were Jean Baudrillard and Jean Nouvel, Paul Chemetov and Didier Daeninckx, Henri Gaudin and Jean-Pierre Vernant, Antoine Grumbach and Antoine Bailly, and Henri Ciriani and Olivier Rolin. Hélène Bleskine developed the idea of Urban Passages and organized the dialogues.

1. Destruction

Christian de Portzamparc: When I came back to New York in November, I went to see the Twin Towers site. I was very impressed. In fact, I had gone to see the Twin Towers three months before because I was working for a competition held near the United Nations on the subject of vertical dimension. These towers were so abstract and dizzying that their dimensions were no longer relative to the city. It was no longer possible to know if fifteen hundred feet were very different from two thousand or twenty-five hundred feet. Beyond a certain height, the impact on the immediate environment is the same; the building becomes incommensurable while, of course, it transforms the skyline of the city. These towers, which had been an unmatched technical achievement that had transformed Manhattan, seemed to have strangely fallen down from the sky. Yet, they had been of relatively little interest among architects. The towers were beyond commentary, and, in the past as well as in the present, people had not realized the work required to conceive and build them. The architect I. M. Pei took me to see the engineer who built them, Leslie Robertson, and we spent an afternoon and a morning together. This meeting was fascinating. Robertson showed and explained to us the steps in the conception, manufacture, and engineering that went into making the facades. He also showed us the drawings of the assembly process, the building site, the research, the psychosensory tests on the motions of the buildings, their resistance to winds, etc. He was visibly very affected by the destruction of the towers. On Ground Zero, they were working on the demolition. The ground was still smoldering. We were seeing the ground itself. The concrete and steel had exploded, had melded, and now soil was visible again; one could plant radishes in it. At three thousand degrees, everything melts. There were a few beams still surviving here and there, and then just the ground. All this matter has been transformed, packed, pushed down twenty-five yards into the ground. And the size of this site was impressive, so huge. It gave a strong physical impression. The towers were so tall that it was difficult to have a precise impression of their dimensions. They had been experienced as a whole, an ensemble that had suddenly appeared and had consecrated the fact of Manhattan's symbolic greatness. Having had the opportunity to measure the size of the floors by looking at the studies Robertson made prior to the actual building, I became aware of the nature of these building events so outside all known dimensions. There is a photo, taken from a distance, from Brooklyn, at dusk, in which the towers are completely transparent. The sky is red and the sun filters through every floor. They are two immense cages. Curiously, we see two hollow, luminous bodies that the gaze travels through.

Robertson explained to us that Yamasaki, the architect, suffered from vertigo and that this motivated the structural conception of the facade with vertical steel support beams surrounding very large, open floors, thus acting as a filter to prevent the sensation of being right in the sky. Some people have tended to forget that these buildings were amazing technical achievements; they were the purest, the most abstract, and the biggest that existed at the time. Thus they were seen as symbols, as ideas that were almost spiritual. And suddenly, there was a hole, smoke. The most striking pictures are those broadcast just after the plane crash, particularly the bird's-eye view taken from the helicopter, an unreal picture revealing people standing at the edge of the gaping hole. The temperature is rising, they are looking down. . . . Robertson told us they had calculated the impact of a B-52 on those buildings and concluded that they would remain standing. They did this because in 1948, a B-52 had grazed the Empire State Building. It had chipped it; the building had been repaired. The event took on a mythical aura. It was possible for a plane to enter a tower! So they calculated the impact of a B-52 and took it into account. He showed us comparisons of the force of the impact with the speed and weight of present-day planes. On September 11, the first plane crashed into the first tower with a force ten times greater than the potential impact a B-52 would have had on the same building. And the size of the fuel tank caused an explosion and temperature twenty times greater. I saw something almost archaic and medieval in this attack as, suddenly, in our era of economic and virtual numbers, we are seeing the violent return of the symbols of the church spire, the dungeon, and the catapult. Robertson told us how the towers had been planned and chosen: the Port Authority wanted to have the tallest towers in the world built so as to rekindle economic activity in the southern portion of New York City and explicitly wanted to turn them into a symbol. It was pretty rare at the time to actually "program" a symbol. This helps foster my impression that this is the repetition of an old story, that of the towers and walls of the towns of San Giminiano and Sienna that were felled by a shower of enormous cannon balls to bring fear to the inhabitants.

Phillipe Sollers: Is it perhaps an Islamic dream to build mosques taller than churches? I remember a text on Mark Rothko titled "New York's Mosques." And then there's the fact that the second plane crashed into the Morgan Stanley floor, which is the bank of fiscal shelters, a bank that was doing poorly already in the summer of 2001.

C.d.P. This bank's situation two months before had bode ill for the future and presaged a time of lean cows for a number of corporations. As a result, Bernard Arnaud had to stop the work on the site of a second small tower we were building on

Madison Avenue, next to the first one. This happened just before September 11.

P.S. Money, mosques, towers,[1] caves.

C.d.P. Deadly caves, these holes in the towers. We are witnessing a return to something originary. And this event happened while we were still fascinated by a new imaginary globalization; everyone sang hymns to the virtual, said that space no longer mattered, but without seeing that we were stalked by a return to archaism in its most violent form. There was something virtual about the Twin Towers precisely because their dimensions existed beyond familiar scales, beyond human references.

Last April, I came to New York for an urbanism competition on the site next to the UN. I wanted to rethink how tall a tower could be. I noticed that once it rose to eight hundred or one thousand feet, it becomes almost impossible to estimate its height; it no longer cast a shadow; it is in the sky. So why not two thousand feet rather than fifteen hundred? The abstract nature of these towers doesn't negate the human body but displaces it spatially and mentally. It is no longer possible to conjure up a mental representation of the space that these buildings deploy; we can no longer quite imagine what it is. I like to compare the size of their surface on the ground to a Paris neighborhood. I think that the Twin Towers would take up half of an arrondissement. So should we keep on building towers? Two planes crashing on a horizontal neighborhood of a European city would also do major damage. The problem posed by a tower is that everybody is in the same place. There's panic, stairs, etc. But the people on the seventieth floor of the Twin Towers did have time to make it down safely. This calls for praise for the engineer and for Yamasaki!

P.S. How old is he?

C.d.P. He must be seventy years old by now, and he was thirty-five when he conceived of this project around 1966.

P.S. The towers were built in 1970–71.

C.d.P. He is a private and rather self-effacing man, very affected by the attack, very much a professional, and now everybody is asking him: Why? How? Everybody is concerned with the way the towers and their resistance were calculated.

P.S. Since September 11 there has been much discussion on whether the towers should be rebuilt.

C.d.P. Yes, and they asked our opinion. Some people are thinking that only a memorial should be built. I think that the idea of a memorial is almost decadent. It means conceding a timeless victory to the attack. Yes, we must remember. The victims should be remembered at the site, but it's not the Shoah. Of course, something should be rebuilt, but what? From an optimistic point of view, more abstract, stronger, higher towers should be built. After these past forty years, we should logically be able to build them stronger, more impressive, more modern. Otherwise history would be going backward! So how high should they be? This sort of race for maximum height is a bit silly. It is not possible to outdo the abstraction of these towers. We know that their power stemmed precisely from their extreme abstraction. Next to them, the rest of New York seems old, heavy, and dark.

P.S. Simply less beautiful.

C.d.P. Yes, less beautiful. Still, the towers were not hailed as an architectural masterpiece; they were simply a phenomenon that fitted with the times. They transcended this because of their immense size. It was this dimension that gave their abstraction so much power.

P.S. In the film made by André S. Labarthe,[2] there's a still that I would love to find and save. We were in New York and were coming back on the Long Island ferry at the end of the afternoon, and we could see the towers in the distance. When sailing into New York, the city looks like a toy made of very small building blocks, and the two towers fit between my two fingers.

C.d.P. These towers brought an extraordinary set of questions on the human urban dimension—landscape, society, civilization— but these were implicit questions because in a way we no longer thought about them. Silence surrounded them. Silence and the blue of the sky. It was as if they were a last architectural gesture, on the scale of a whole city, a whole island. Later on, we entered a different era in which the preoccupation with erecting fifteen-hundred-foot-high towers seemed less essential and the bottom line became the primary factor, in spite of plans to build towers in Asia that would reach three thousand feet in height. And then, the virtual image became dominant.

P.S. The Twin Towers were a last hurrah.

C.d.P. Once that symbol was destroyed, there came the realiza-tion that they had had a quasi-spiritual dimension, that they were architecturally beyond human references. The sublime advocated by Boullée had truly been reached.[3] These towers were an irreversible event in the aesthetic history of modernity. Any work done on this site that would negate this reference would seem to be a denial of this dimension.

P.S. So you don't think that anything could be built in their place?

C.d.P. What I mostly think is that if we were to *not* rebuild these towers we would experience them forever as a lost object. But it might be impossible, and maybe even ridiculous, to rebuild identical ones. This leaves me perplexed. If identical towers were built, this would amount to fetishism. There hasn't been any fundamental progress made in construction techniques, but we could make them better, stronger, more luminous. We need to rethink urban life on the ground, a life that was cold and sad. So it is crucial and necessary to rethink life in those structures—air, breathing, circulation. Of course, we could build two-thousand-foot towers instead of fifteen-hundred-foot towers. Beyond two thousand feet, construction poses complicated problems involving the subsoil that are very expensive to resolve. Finally, at this point of the island, the proportion was perfect, as was the relation to the site. No, I wouldn't build them any taller.

P.S. Were you struck by journalists' comments about the fact that we weren't shown images of the dead bodies?

C.d.P. Of course.

P.S. There was a fellow telling what happened. He was running and was told, hurry, hurry, and don't look to the left, but he looked anyway, just as in the Bible, and he saw things that he'll remember for a long time. But there was a deliberate intent to avoid showing bodies. Are you aware of this aspect of the issue?

C.d.P. You and I already talked about this when discussing the death penalty in the United States and the abstraction of death. The camera crews explained that they wanted to avoid filming the dead, death, sensationalizing it.

P.S. No exposed corpses, no remains, no piles of dead bodies.

C.d.P. An impossible mourning.

P.S. We can go even further and talk of a taboo of death. These are two great puritanical systems, one American and the other Islamic, that come together in the violent negation of the body.

C.d.P. And on September 11, the very image of the tragedy was first of all these abstract towers, pierced, brought down. There was a total disjunction between the external image and internal reality. They crumbled down in a sort of spectacle that was literally unbelievable, gripping because we knew that there were thousands of bodies inside. But the event was absolutely spectacular, calculated to occur at the time of day when most of the planet could see it live.

P.S. We saw some people who jumped.

C.d.P. Let us imagine that the terrorists missed their target and that the planes crashed in New Jersey. Of course there would have been major damage, and of course media from the whole world would have been there; there would have been horrible spectacles of gaping houses and corpses; they would have filmed it, and we would have seen "all" because the visual field would have been in the open. *Paris Match* would have shown pictures of the bodies. It would have been an atrocious spectacle, but much less important, less humiliating than the attack on the towers, even if there would have been an equal number of tragic deaths. What happened in Manhattan on that day, the destruction of the towers, touches us in other ways. Even though science fiction had predicted it, it was unimaginable, and this is what problematizes all we had taken for granted.

P.S. That's the religious aspect of the question.

C.d.P. The people who were in charge of predictions, of planning for defense, had not been able to conceive of an event of such magnitude. They were thinking of space-based wars; they were focused on protecting American soil from aerial attacks. American cities must have seemed untouchable to them. The September 11 event broke the illusion that America could be absolutely protected.

P.S. On a background of caves.

C.d.P. On one side towers and on the other caves: fullness and emptiness.

P.S. Yes, I can see that. We can't help seeing these two towers over a background of mountains and caverns, as in a somewhat surrealistic montage. And this involves erasing all that stands between the two—well, just about all. So it forces upon us an injunction to maintain as secondary everything that separates them. New York mosques, why not? Or the Strasbourg cathedral since it appears that an attack on it has been thwarted. So it does seem legitimate to bring up the religion card. It's a religious story.

C.d.P. The whole of a face of the world—that of the making of cities, the material construction of the buildings, their meaning, their symbolic dimension, their lastingness—has been as if veiled, forgotten, or outmoded for the last thirty years in the face of the dominant yet fleeting issues of the circulation of money. We are in the midst of another abstraction, this time an economic one. But after September 11, a terrible physical reality has brutally come back to remind us of its existence. For the inhabitants of New York, for all of us as well, it is traumatic.

P.S. We are all New Yorkers, though not necessarily Americans.

C.d.P. There was always the city of civilization, the core city. There was Rome, Constantinople, Paris in the nineteenth century, then it was New York starting in Ford's time, the twentieth century, the Empire State Building, economic domination. I remember the question the Japanese were asking us in the 1980s during a conference about urbanism: what will be *the* city of the twenty-first century? Will it be Los Angeles or Tokyo?

P.S. Shanghai?

C.d.P. Shanghai or Tokyo? They were talking about the decline of New York and the move to the Pacific economic sphere, about the geographical handicap suffered by New York, at the time bogged in its problems of density and pollution; they were showing the impossibility of its development and economic renewal. In fact, New York has kept on being the world city. You were saying we are facing a religious event. What other city could play this guiding role? You were ironic when you mentioned the Vatican. It is not only economic power that is at stake; it is a sacred dimension, and obviously it is the fanatics who are unveiling it: what is a city that outreaches cities and represents both legacy and the installation of the concentrated future time?

P.S. Still the cave. But we shouldn't forget that New York is the city that sprang out of the destruction of Europe. It's the enormous symbolic stake at play in this fact because of the ruin, the devastation, of Berlin. Of course there are other megalopolises, and there will yet be others, but perhaps never as symbolically charged. New York is the answer to a certain type of massive destruction. Here we are facing a question, we are facing *the* metaphysical question itself, that is, the religiosity inhabiting every metaphysics, and God knows it exists with a particular virulence here. This is part of the issues raised at present by the end results of nihilism, and there's no doubt that this is having a massive impact on religion. This being said, I'm not sure that the target was really New York. It was the Twin Towers! You're right, a destruction in New York, even of extraordinary import, would have been a direct attack on the city, but here I think we have touched something else, something that is part of New York but that also goes beyond it. The attack on the Pentagon didn't have the same impact. And all this happened on a background of money, a huge amount of money. Suddenly the emergence of the islands—something interesting not only from a geographical viewpoint but also from that of architecture: what is happening in the Bahamas, in Guernsey, in the Cook islands? These towers were the embodiment of the spread of these fiscal paradises. We should have the courage to say that though the spectacle was horrible, it was also extraordinarily beautiful. Very beautiful.[4] These images will make up an extraordinary object, we won't be able to leave them behind. The same goes for the figure of the "great criminal" that was constructed immediately after September 11, that is, Bin Laden. He is obviously going to occupy an impressive symbolic place among famous criminals. The issue is to know how the proofs of his eventual death will be presented. He is already "dead," we agree on that. But how to present his corpse? A mistake that should be avoided: a Christlike presentation, the Renaissance tableau, or the presentation of the body in the Che Guevara mode. We shouldn't repeat this. We would then find ourselves in a system of visual representations implying a Christlike death. So how are we going to prove that Bin Laden is dead? Right now, everyone is preoccupied with the question of how to present his corpse. Should it be photographed, should it be in a casket? Does he disappear under the rubble?

C.d.P. It's not certain that he is dead. But you claim he's dead.

P.S. He is virtually, potentially dead. We are not imagining that he would be tried and executed somewhere in the United States, which is not likely, the more so in that we don't know how this trial would be held. A number of embarrassing facts could be revealed in between two citations from the Prophet. But he will occupy a choice place in the history of famous criminals. He has just entered the gallery, and he'll be in focus. Perhaps the corpse will disappear after all. At any rate, there will be a legend. Couched in an odious and grotesque genre, we can't help laugh at it, a nasty laugh triggered by a slapstick skit in which we see Bin Laden bearded and brandishing his Kalashnikov in front of a cardboard cave and suddenly grabbing a microphone and singing "New York, New York"—we can't help but laugh. What interests me right now is the difference in potential between caves and towers. So what will the artists do?

C.d.P. This difference seems enormous to us because it carries the aura of all the technology that separates them, but on another plane, it is the same game, the same world—the exposed symbolic tower, the hidden cave, the cannon, the cannonball or the plane having become a cannonball, the collapsing. There is an obsessive worldwide activity having to do with money, a permanent ritual that turns money into a kind of substitute for the religious, a reason for being. On September 11, many corporate leaders lost everything, but we know that at that moment, they were only thinking of the dead. They were forgetting money and the twenty-four-hour-a-day stock exchange, otherwise unstoppable, a clerical service ensuring the perpetual transmission of a state of the world . . .

P.S. . . . of which you can't see the peripheries.

C.d.P. This stock market is something that might be taking over the place held by religion.

P.S. Or it might be its more and more evident manifestation at the moment when Metaphysics completes its journey. What can a society that has an absolute respect for money become? That is the reason, when it comes to building a concert hall, to prefer an architect who knows music rather than B-52s—this seems to me logical. The architect's services are going to be increasing solicited by the great cities of the world.

C.d.P. This with the aim of giving visibility to a part of the money. Big banks, for instance, where there's a lot of money, always had a sense of the ceremonial. Today, ritualization is more contained, more prudent.

P.S. Pei's tower in Hong Kong is a bank.

C.d.P. Do you remember when we were talking about a project by the Hearst group and of the neo-Gothic salon where they received me in which there hung the portrait that Orson Welles used as a model for Citizen Kane? The high ceiling, the large table, the verticality of it all, the portraits, and the stained glass windows fostered the idea of a dynasty's palace. These things from the 1920s purposely carry a historical reference; they embodied the transmission of values. The word "values" has both ethical and monetary meanings. It no longer functions quite the same way because technological efficiency is now of primary import. The image of technology has taken over the place held by the symbolic.

P.S. Can you see that in the gallery of the famous criminals of our time, we are now facing a billionaire? We are dealing with an unusual case: Hitler was not a billionaire at the outset; Stalin and Mao even less. We are dealing with a billionaire who is functioning in caverns. This also entails a lot of questions that are difficult to answer because they unfold in the shadows, in opacity, as for instance poppy culture in Afghanistan. I don't know if you have heard the latest information: the Taliban is collecting the Koranic tithe on the poppies.

C.d.P. It seems they keep it at a reasonable level and respect the producers!

P.S. So, business has been bad, the peasants held on to their crop, and during the last few months, addicts in Saint Petersburg couldn't keep their date with their suppliers. There was a shortage of heroin, and they were forced to use other drugs. In the past few weeks, the market has rebounded. We can keep track of the traffic as it goes through Russia, Sweden, and then to the United States. There is a considerable resurgence going on with enormous sums at stake; this is only one example among others. We could map the same route for arms, food, etc. But there is a point that seems just as interesting to me: the old man of the mountain, the hash lord, transformed himself into a billionaire in his cave so as to attack in these towers the erectile concentration of money, which is indeed a very strong symbol and not only in the United States. I can see that the Twin Towers provoked a religious act. The will to destroy a given symbolic form at a given time is anchored in the impulse of death, as if God himself were taking vengeance on a representation that displeased him. So these two forms, these twin towers—I said that I had intensely experienced them, the question being to know who had been there when something had been there, and not only whether there was already something "already there" but who was present at the moment when something did happen? This sort of question can lead to dissertations just as it can lead to the sort of texts that might endure in the history of humankind for the simple reason that the one who was there *was there.* There was a witness. Think of the Evangelists, for instance. Let's assume that someone was there. It was such an event! That goes for the Koran as well, the words of the Prophet are real in Islamic culture, etc. Who was there at the moment of the Paris Commune? Who was there in 1851, on December 2, 3, 4, and 5 in Paris? For three days Victor Hugo was alone in the midst of an important historical event. The coup d'état happened when everyone else was in bed, but he was witness to it. He was there. And afterward, this presence led to writings and rewritings of history. So who has really *lived* these towers? That is the issue. They are no longer there. They were there. Who was there while they were there? Who thought what about them at the moment when they were there, in a way that was not linked to one's own habits, to the towers' function, to the fact that one was working in them? In a way, who was inhabiting them? Who found that they were inhabited by something else than was believed? There are two shapes that I found interesting from the outset. There was the bullion shape, the gold bars question, the standard they represented. The second shape was that of the microphone, the radio microphone. The shapes looked like they were made for something to go through them, and then we saw that that something was B-52s. Also radium bars, something that irradiates, that is completely atomic in a certain manner. From this viewpoint, it is an achievement in which the unconscious of technology and of science produced an admirable masterpiece. There are other achievements, abstract ones, as you said, for architecture, but few of them have had the same power in their application. All this appeared to me in a vital manner when I wandered around these towers, when I had my visions of New York and I was writing *Paradis*. And now, what are we going to replace them with?

C.d.P. They were located in the oldest part of New York City, the part that didn't yet have a structure, that was laid out irregularly, not with straight angles.

P.S. It's the duality that is interesting, two columns.

C.d.P. But I am also speaking here of the relationship with all the rest, with Manhattan; they are interesting in relation to all the rest, as an intervention for the island, in the island. This intervention, by modifying Manhattan at one point, at two points, transformed the whole of its physiognomy and imposed a new face on it.

P.S. There is something that I don't understand why it has not been commented on at more length: it is the parallel between the blowing up of the statues of the Buddha and the destruction of the Twin Towers. Do you remember the Buddha statues in their recesses in the rock face? There were two of them, and they blew them up with dynamite. Just this should have been enough to trigger retaliatory bombings. But probably because there was still the possibility that Mullah Omar could undertake a certain type of negotiation about the relations of power in the region, no one did a thing. And here we have the whole of the American–Russian circus as it played out this affair. Let's not forget the essential picture of the beginning of the third millennium: Bush and Putin wearing blue silk Chinese jackets, dressed like girls by Yiang Zemin who himself was dressed in orange—Chinese humor. Finally, we must ask the question of what should be done about the already there of the Twin Towers. So what would you replace them with?

C.d.P. The abstract form of the towers, their location at the head of the island, their outsized dimension, the function of trading[5] in the Wall Street district, all this converged with the unconscious sacred aspect of this architecture. At the time of their building, these aspects were introduced in terms of performance, square feet, functionality, and dynamics, since people did not like to talk of anything else. The notion of symbol was alien to functionalist discourse.

P.S. But it was a magnificent achievement.

C.d.P. Any attempt to reconstruct them from another aesthetic viewpoint would be seen as weak for the very reason that it would be aesthetic. Since they were sacred, the temptation is to rebuild them in the identical mode, as we would have done for the Gabriel building in Paris on the Place de la Concorde if it had been bombed during the war. However, by doing this we get the impression that the future forbids us to be inventive or that we are being fetishistic.

P.S. Unlike our own practice, the Japanese don't think that the dimension of the sacred is tied to uniqueness or originality. They rebuild certain temples every sixty years. The exact replica of the temple is built next to the old one, and then the old one is dismantled. In Japan, there is no respect for the materials used originally, for the real body, for what is of crucial import to us. It is our Christian legacy. The only necessity for them is to respect the form, the space as it was originally conceived.

P.S. So who will be brave enough to see that it is sacred? Why wouldn't we want it to be sacred? The sacred is not fetishism. Some people imagine that by not rebuilding the Twin Towers they would become sacred and at the same time so would the victims. But I don't think so. Frankly, I would rebuild identical ones.

C.d.P. It's an idea. I don't know when the notion that only the original material is of value has become a dogma. At the time of Viollet-le-Duc, there was a great debate on this.

P.S. I am intrigued that no one dares think to rebuild identically. And there are strong possibilities that hiding behind this stance are uneasiness, awkward feelings, heaviness, a relationship with death that is murky, to say the least.

C.d.P. If the rebuilding is identical, does it mean that we remain stuck to the tragedy, or on the contrary, do we recognize in the towers a sacred dimension that would then be magnified?

P.S. Sacred? Poetic?

C.d.P. I say "sacred" so as to get people to grasp the nature of the heart of a city, but I still put it in quotation marks.

P.S. Well, let's say "sacred" in quotation marks.

C.d.P. Every time you imagine something else where the towers used to be, this image has a sort of weakness in relation to the extreme abstraction they used to be . . .

P.S. . . . and still are.

C.d.P. Another view is to build bigger, but that would be a child-ish impulse. The question is no longer totally meaningful. The towers were at once modern and archaic.

P.S. Identical towers have to be built. That is the only possible way to show respect for the victims.

C.d.P. The base of the towers was not functional. It was cold and windy there—it never worked. It is something that should be modified. But there were the towers. I am sure that they couldn't be built in a more abstract form, or that if they were built in a less abstract one, something would be lost. Something else would then have to be gained. These towers were above and beyond what a work of art can be. They were, and this is pretty rare, a conjunction at a given moment between modern history and architecture, between business at the beginning of its globalization and the technique of the skyscraper at its apogee.

P.S. So the question is quite important: in other words, do we become decadent if we don't rebuild identically? Isn't this where shame could lie?

C.d.P. There is the risk of rendering another sort of thing sacred—time itself. At present and since the sixties, from that moment of apogee that was the construction of the Twin Towers, the notion of patrimony has come to the fore. From the moment a building is more than one hundred years old, it becomes a subject of preservation, reconstruction, reparations. But progress still remains important. And with it the strong desire to unite time and its becoming, to not lock ourselves up in myth. There is thus a sort of hysteria. There will be the notion that by rebuilding we would be going backward, that it is fake.

P.S. It is not identical rebuilding that makes it a fake because if this were true, it would mean that at that moment, a certain dimension of time had gone forever and that indeed building something different would mean going backward.

C.d.P. We conceive of time as narrow, as a vector. There was the same discussion in East Berlin, after the wall fell: should the castle be rebuilt, the city itself as it used to be, or should something else be constructed? Everything that is older than a century is "museumified." An absurd example would be Montmartre if the Sacré-Coeur basilica were to be destroyed. The popular viewpoint would be that it should be rebuilt the way it was; it is Paris, after all. And that would be considered seriously.

P.S. You can argue this because the Sacré-Coeur is built over the martyrs of the Commune uprising, thus it is a monument of the civil war.

C.d.P. And it is also a monument that is generally looked upon as aesthetically rather unsuccessful.

P.S. It mostly carries an extraordinary historical weight; to not rebuild it would mean that the history of France has passed beyond (not likely to happen in the near future) all the problems linked to the French civil war, that it has left behind all of the skeletons in the closets.

C.d.P. But it is confusing: I think the inhabitants are attached to Montmartre almost for reasons of urban physiognomy. They don't want the neighborhood to change. These are animal reasons, the ancestors' trees, fear. We can well wonder if the consensus over the need to rebuild history condemns our epoch to weak thinking, to modest ambition, to an incredible fetishism of the past, even as we are living in a time when economy is relegating architecture and the city in the making to secondary concerns, memory games, nonessential, nonvital rituals. This is because they do not manifest the meaning carried by the circulation of money; they stand instead for a time that has regressed from the future. Take, for instance, the Eiffel tower. It would have to be rebuilt identically, of course. Two years ago, there was an architectural project that would have outlined in space the spires of Notre Dame as they had been originally conceived but never built. The spires were planned to be very high, magnificent tapered pyramids as high as the actual height of Notre Dame and its towers. The complete plan is never shown, it is very different. Notre Dame is an interrupted project.

P.S. Here you're touching on Notre Dame of Paris, thus Victor Hugo, for instance.

C.d.P. The architect Alain Renk proposed this temporary installation for the year 2000. The shape of the spires was to be outlined with very fine carbon lines and would have been installed for a year. I found the project of revealing what had been conceived originally for these spires interesting, particularly in that it would have been only through a luminous outline in space, as a sort of geometrical object.

P.S. Temporarily.

C.d.P. So, if Notre Dame were destroyed . . .

P.S. It would have to be rebuilt identically. Just like the Fenice opera house. Do you remember when Nietzsche broke down in tears because he thought the Tuileries in Paris had been destroyed? If the Twin Towers are not rebuilt identical to the destroyed ones, it is death that would triumph.

2. Can We Think without Language?

C.d.P. I would like us to think about the following: how do we think with and without language? This question preoccupies me a lot. In fact, this is really a question about the nature of architecture.

In a debate, I was led to explain my projects of open islands in urbanism and to expand on my vision of the ages of the city, and I noticed that this made historians strangely upset. I realized that what I was telling them seemed to them provocative, simplifying, and that in their view, when you come down to it, there is something in scientific knowledge, as they call it, that anesthetizes us and that makes the world seem flat to us, while the world is really a hallucination—reality is a hallucination. When I spoke of what I call Age II of the city, of this surprising, unpredictable, transformative moment of the modern city, of the adventure of the century, one of them replied: "But this time, did it really begin? Did it really exist?"[1]

We can see in this attitude that the greatest evidence can escape us. What I wanted to explain there, and which seemed very clear to me, was that we have to have visions, emotions, and enthusiasms and that we should analyze them, transmit them, think with, and question ourselves with them. It is something existing in between emotion and knowledge because it is with this that one does architecture, with visions and not with descriptions. Then I wondered about the fact that when we are doing architecture, an architectural project, we are not thinking with language. I think through schemas and impressions; I draw fragments; I glue a couple of photographs. I don't know where I am, but I am not in a discourse, I am not in a thought that could be spoken, that needs to be spoken and then translated into a form.

The organization of Western knowledge, the concepts used in education, art, architecture, etc., separate, render impermeable, two domains: that of scientific knowledge, with its texts and programs, logos, and its authority; and the domain of forms, that is, of the people who put things into forms and are aware that after this forming comes the work on matter itself. Architecture would be located somewhere between thought and matter. But it is seen as being somewhat bogged down by matter, and so the question arises as to whether it is possible to think with it. Yet, we just need to look at the world that is counting, counting, but doesn't seem to do a lot of thinking. Traditionally, architecture was artistic, sensible, intuitive, a gesture. This brings us back to a vision of the Beaux Arts, a vision that teaches us nothing. I hold, on the contrary, that there must be thinking when we are drawing, photographing, filming. Yes, there has been thinking. So how does it work?

I wanted to talk with you, Philippe, because you live in language and at the same time vision is very strong in you; you are a seer, a writer who sees. You state, "The more I write, the more I see." I am reading here what you wrote on Cézanne:

"Very few individuals can *see*. It is very strange but that's the way it is. So it is not surprising if the least spectacle has so great an effect on the majority of people. The yelling, the programs, the money, the circus, the television, the power—this is normal in what we could call humankind's endemic narcissistic psychosis. I brought someone's attention to a flowerbed of pansies, and he told me: 'I don't see the flowers.' That was a brave admission; at least he wasn't pretending. 'I don't see the flowers' is a defense reaction against nothingness, just as it is if you endow a rose with the least bit of a *why*. Why something rather than nothing? But Cézanne says, 'I owe you the truth in painting, and I will tell it to you.' 'You will then see that you are not seeing.'" And you add, "You will then see that you are not seeing. You will then learn that you are spending your time refusing to see and to know."[2] You insist on this extraordinary statement by Cézanne: "As sensations make up the base of what I'm doing, I believe myself to be impenetrable." And a bit further on you write: "I cannot imagine seeing a Cézanne in one take. I sense that, in order to return it to vision, I have to think it almost point by point, stroke by stroke, plane by plane, slowly, fast, as if I would never be able to complete it as an ensemble. This ensemble must 'rise' with me like the way it was painted. Like this bridge that seems so straightforward," the Maincy bridge near Meulan, the painting of "this bridge that seems so straightforward, just like that, 'a landscape.' It will take a certain length of *time* (and this *time* is space itself) before I see the way the two slender tree trunks in the foreground intertwine at the same height as the bridge's span, which is 'behind,' or the fluid jet of the branches, above left. Little by little I will undergo an inverse apprenticeship, self-critical of my incessant manner of getting rid of the depth of 'nature,' that is, of visible thought, of myself for the benefit of a false self. *One cannot see* Cézanne, this is what Cézanne convinces us of. Will itself, the will within oneself, prevents us from seeing."

And you add: "It is precisely because of the possibility of simplifying *The Card Players* that it cannot be simplified. The pocket of the player on the right is too low; I mentally correct it without thinking. These legs under the table, I will turn them into sensible legs even though they are impressions of legs. The arm of the player on the left, I will raise it to his shoulder, and I would be wrong because that arm, as if it were external to the body, added to it, lives a long trajectory by itself before arriving to his hands holding the white cards" (they are white so as to say among other things that the whole of the painting is a card game: Cézanne's canvasses do not flow from Descartes, but they *are* cards or maps, though neither those of a café game nor of geography).³ And thus the players' table takes on its fabulous autonomy and so does the back of the chair of the player on the left, and the hat, the pipe, the background, all start to exist in the time of this painting and no other. I am thus renouncing the optical grip. *Optical grip.* You wrote before this that Cézanne always resisted being grabbed into someone's clutches. "I renounce the optical grip, the deadly vulgarity of the 'I have seen'; in reality I no longer see anything. I am thinking about seeing, *which is entirely different.*"⁴

According to our Western tradition, from the time of the ancient Greeks, the *cogito,* there is no thought outside of language because language is its sole vehicle. It is through language that we succeeded in freeing ourselves from the muck of the multitude of sensations enveloping us, from prejudgments and fears, in order to name, classify, choose; this is what the rational thought that came into being in ancient Greece holds. Language extracts us from the sensible world and spares us from having to experience or reexperience or mimic a thing, an affect, so as to be able to imagine it. The aim is to short-circuit experience; it is thus that the concept comes into being. We still have this preconceived idea that intelligence requires abstraction.

Rousseau wrote that he loved geometry—this at a time when they were still using figures—and he was bothered and irritated by what he called the fashion of reasoning in geometry through analysis without using figures. In fact, Euclidian geometry is no more because we now know everything in it. The figure has been completely explored. Mathematics has evolved in such a way that mathematicians have freed themselves from the figure, from sensible proofs, to arrive at more and more abstractions. In the 1960s, with Saussure and linguistics, language became a generic system. Everybody was grabbing it, including sociology as well as architects. Lacan explains that "the unconscious is structured like a language." There's more to language than what we expect from it; it is more than an instrument of communication. It is a matrix. It would be interesting to find out whether language is the absolute condition for thought, to find out how we think outside of science. I believe that the poet thinks differently. What is the ground from which someone can subvert language? I am thinking of Rimbaud. He seems to suddenly get out of language, to go further, much further than what language can say. An architect has the impression that everything that is place, space, cannot be said, or only in a reduction that is coded, limited, and insufficient though useful.

To give an example, Erwin Panofsky wrote a book on Gothic architecture during the 1960s. It was a brilliant demonstration aimed at making us understand that Gothic architecture originated in scholastic thought. He describes very well the how of it: how the Gothic blueprint was inspired by the classifications of Saint Thomas Aquinas's *Summa Theologica* and all the precepts of the Abbé Suger. And then, immersed in the movement, as if we were listening to Champollion,[5] we get a practical demonstration of the why of the forms: there had previously been a text. There was a thought, and this is why we have an aesthetic. And yet we can't help thinking that something essential has been lost along the way, along the course of the analysis. In Gothic architecture this idea of verticality, of light coming from on high, from heaven, is an aesthetic ambition and a technique for lighting, for light, for visibility. The idea of building much higher, with big windows and stained glass filtering light, could not have been born in Romanesque churches because it is the invention of counterthrusts that made it possible to lighten and to go higher. We have here the conjunction of an essential technical invention, an architectural idea, a desire to make the likes of Cluny and Tournus and Silvacane outmoded—all backed by an idea according to which God is light, and God is on high; thus one must let the light come down from as high as possible. But this light and this freedom from weight are not at all simple facts of language, are they? Panofsky's book shows that the program, the *Summa,* dictated the organization of the plan of the cathedrals to the extent that we are led to believe that words would have been sufficient and that Gothic architecture came out of a discourse and, in a way, is its material translation. Of course, this view jelled in a time focused on theories, systems, nascent computer science, and another future for architecture, one that would be textual, digital, etc. Programs could soon be entered into computers that would spew out plans, go faster, and make us smarter. There were believers. But something was obviously getting lost.

Roland Barthes also took some interest in the matter. He wrote of the possibility of a semiology of architecture that would describe the syntagmatic and paradigmatic order that could be extracted from a building, etc. I had the opportunity of discussing this with him. He had come to participate in a thesis defense that must have dealt with a work in the field of semiology. I told him, "We have the impression that with language, here, something escapes us, something is concealed, and that something is space." And he basically answered, "It's true, it makes sense, but perhaps the essential is lost." He was passing through all fields. He was in the process of writing *The Pleasure of the Text*. At that time, he had already distanced himself from the idea of a general semiotics. I was telling him that space escapes language. So what is your impression of the way you're thinking? Because my own impression is that I am not necessarily thinking with language.

P.S. *What Is Called Thinking? (Was heisst denken?)* is a major work by Martin Heidegger.[6] Its title ought rather be translated as "what calls for thinking?" I always found Heidegger's courses extraordinary as they gradually and very cautiously progressed toward the theme "we are not yet thinking." It is a notion that could be expected to make everyone indignant. After all, I think because in principle I am. I am even supposed to be constantly thinking. So in Heidegger, there would be a proposition of defiance toward this idea. In reality I should rather say: I think, thus I am representing to myself that I am. I am in the representation. It is very interesting to get deeper into what you just told me, because what you have done is no less than give an overall definition of the history of metaphysics, that is, of that which has excluded the poet from the City. It's very explicit in Plato and it is manifest in architecture, of course. So Heidegger has this strange concern—and you will see it is not a question simply of language as it is rooted in the functioning of the human being—to define that which is the opposite of thought, that which occurs by the force of the will. The will, yes. That is what the obstacle to thinking is according to him; it is what he calls the spirit of revenge. And he quotes Nietzsche's statement, "Revenge itself [is] the will's revulsion against time and its 'It was.'"[7] This spirit of revenge would be constantly at play in the will's will, that is, in the will to power that is the end of metaphysics. In this view, because of the will's resentment against time itself, the will would have been at all times preoccupied by the desire to avenge itself from the past. We cannot deny that, from this viewpoint, the twentieth century has offered us grandiose manifestations of this spirit of vengeance in all its forms. Well, this is so in architecture, too. You were talking earlier about an overall plan that would equalize humankind. We can see that the greatest architectural schemes—and you'll certainly have things to say about Le Corbusier's utopia—insist on taking the mass of humankind and make it inhabit places where the equal sign must function as a form of constant and collective surveillance.

On the other hand, architecture thought from the perspective of a multiple singularity can be encountered in the greatest inventions of leaps in architecture throughout time. Today, we are able to attempt clarifying this. Why? Because I believe we are at a very particular moment of history. Something is ending in front of our very eyes. Let us suppose that the year is 1897. Zola is about to enter the Panthéon, this no more for literary reasons than Hugo did, and no more than Malraux, whose ashes were transferred with pomp. Anyway, it's weird to speak of ashes when it is a coffin that is being carried—much too big for ashes. Well, Zola put all his efforts at the time into obliterating Cézanne's painting objectively. He did this in his famous 1886 book *L'Oeuvre*[8] in which he looks upon Cézanne as a madman, a failure, someone who commits suicide because in the end he paints in a way that cannot be a part of the historical representation of the human species as Zola conceived it in terms of indefinite progress. Cézanne, though unknown, holds on; he continues to paint. He even creates more and more extraordinary things, among others, his *Les grandes baigneuses*[9] at the end, which moreover have an absolutely visible architectural intention that did not escape you. In the book *Généalogie de la forme*,[10] Cézanne makes his appearance when you confide something about your drawings and your passion for drawing. And not only him—there's Lao-Tzu. What interests me here is that you are writing about your groping with drawing, with painting, which opened up suddenly onto architecture. You use the magnificent expression *architectural landscapes*. It is a reverie, a groping in the dark. There are bags, pillows, and suddenly moldings and posts make their appearance, as if the drawing was a phantasm, a hallucination. You wrote a very beautiful text that clearly proves that this is first of all an internal experience: "In the train from Paris to Rennes, 1 June 1973. Today I am the porter, the transporter of acuteness: it has come to me after hours of rain and the dull accumulation of days and things, under the influence of the triangle and the arc of the circle."[11] Is this the statement of a madman? "Today I am the porter, the transporter of acuteness." This is followed by quite a bit of rambling. "The swift movement of the sail, of plant life, of the empty dress: the nonsolid, the torn. That which brings the stroke into full existence: the fold."[12] I must be dreaming! That's an architect? "Yesterday, I felt the degradation of the impression of plasticity in the film image. Today I'm transporting acuteness. A green triangle of mine is just around each door. In the unavoidable accumulation of hours and things, it is there, a sign of being, invisible and, like the arc of the circle, an instrument of vision, slowing down thought. Light filled with the number one, encompassing the poorly defined obscurities of solar and social systems, left on the verbal scrap heap of metaphysics."[13] I found this very well put. But is it rational? The "verbal scrap heap" of metaphysics, and then, suddenly, I see that you use the expression "gulfs of shadows"[14] without giving the author's name. And of course, since I read Rimbaud, I recognize one of his definitions of the vowel *A*,[15] and I'm thinking that you must have been constantly affected by the notion of the colors of vowels.

I once conducted a small experiment. I wrote a novel in which Rimbaud was mentioned a lot in order to see if the French recognize the colors of the vowels of their language. I assumed everyone knew about this. What are the colors of the vowels invented by Rimbaud? And why did he do this?

I was greatly surprised. The best I found was someone who knew three of them. So I can't go around assuming that everyone knows them. I remember this because I was working on it, and I was affected by it.

Do you see the same colors?

C.d.P. I don't see all the colors the same way. I see *A* as black, *E* as white, *I* red, *O* brown rather than blue, and *U* yellow.[16]

P.S. You are able to say this because Rimbaud had the idea of comparing vowels and colors. So you got the same idea. You just said: "I see *O* brown rather than blue." It's a progression. I could say that I see *A* as blue. But that's not the issue, the issue has to do with the appearance of a concept that happens to be one Rimbaud originated. After that, each person is free to invent his or her language, his or her visual language.

You were asking if the image . . .

C.d.P. It is an amusing mystery. For me it is evidence and absolutely not comparison. I do see vowels, and each is a color. I was fairly young when I read Rimbaud, and it seemed evident to me that colors were linked to vowels. I've read the claim that "he had a toy alphabet in color when he was a child"; it is possible, but I don't believe it. It is probably the sound register of the vowels that brings up the colors. Consonants, between the teeth and the tongue, articulate form.

I first found it amusing to say that I hit the nail with some of his colors but that I saw different ones with certain vowels, that's all. Now I believe that it is much more important than it seemed, this permeating of the colors. It is not just anecdotic.

Likewise, I found a newspaper article I had cut out in the sixties that explained that Rimbaud had accompanied Verlaine to London to the exhibition marking the completion of the great Royal Albert Hall, and that the famous text of the *Illuminations* called "Villes"[17] was a transcription of this vision. And Mallarmé was there as well and wrote a reportage on the exposition. Well, it is interesting, but still outside the subject matter, that *Illuminations* remains out of reach, that it pertains to an entirely different thing, that language is more, is other.

P.S. Well, no reportage at all. I was saying earlier, *A* black, *E* white, *I* red, *U* green, *O* blue . . .

You can make whatever you want of this.

One either has or hasn't the strong sensation that colors are vowels. Vowels are what make the voice come through. What is it that speaks in architecture? Architecture is made to speak of what? Is it to form a gathering? To live? To breathe? To inhabit? And to speak of what? I am struck by the danger that threatened the Cité de la Musique.

Of what does the Cité de la Musique speak? It speaks of its architecture, which is there for music to be in it at the same time as it is a locale. This is one way of putting it. I am just thinking of the historical period, at the end of the nineteenth century. Let us suppose we are in 1887, which might be the same thing. Zola is about to enter the Panthéon; Cézanne is invisible. Rimbaud has been dead for six years; no one knows his writings. It is a period of incredible decadence, poverty, intense cultural misery that will end with the butchery of 1914–18. Afterward, there are breaks. People are noticing: look at this, we are on the list! There are polemics, but those are of no import. And then, there is the return to 1873, 1874, 1875. What happened? It is not impossible to relive the sort of situation linked to violent historical phenomena that is the war of 1870 and the Paris Commune on which so many interpretations have been written. Poetry, in the unique freedom it manifests, should have been automatically linked to either a progressive, socialist, or "illuminist" vision of the world, and thus become itself a program or an illustration of a given social program. This lasted for a very long time. I believe we are at a moment when we can see that this is no longer working. At the time when the great French Revolution was taking place, as the Germans put it, there was another great poet; he was in the margins and thought to be mad. He was called Hölderlin, and he wasn't thinking, like his friend Hegel, for instance, was, of the completion of metaphysics. He thinks differently. Hölderlin's images are of an extraordinary simplicity, the great images of Hölderlin. A century passed before his poems started to be talked about, for example, before Heidegger commented on them. Perhaps they are still not understood or read. It is the same for Rimbaud. Time is deferred, the *left-unsaid of metaphysics* is there in a position of confinement, of exclusion. Why? Because indeed there has been a revolution. But not the one believed to have taken place, not the one that has been co-opted in a sort of countercoup. And then if we gather around May '68, it is indeed because there was a revolution—but not the one spoken about. Perhaps in the countercoup that has been obsessing everyone since then, this is because that is where the specter is. This makes three historical epochs that I offer up to you so as to meditate their architectural consequences, but not only those.

What is it that was imposed in architecture? What is it that was excluded from architecture and from poetry? The French Revolution, the Paris Commune, and 1968, Rimbaud's *Cities*. It is pretty strange that no one, I think, has read *Illuminations* for what it is. That is, as you said, a vision that doesn't find its beginning in the program of metaphysics, that doesn't let itself be brought back to metaphysics's fold. Thus, a poetry that doesn't let itself be brought back to what is usually meant by "poetry." There have been many poetical lies spread the same way propaganda is, including patriotic poetry, political agenda poetry, and ensemble poetry. This stands as the opposite of a vision in which it is no longer possible to discern a difference between the word that reaches its destination and the vision that is already there. Architecture, in my opinion, should be practiced so as to let these Cities exist, after having served all those temples. Cults are transitory, but temples remain. So *Cities*? We have yet to catch up with Rimbaud's following precision:

> The official acropolis outdoes the most colossal conceptions of modern barbarity: impossible to describe the opaque light produced by the immutably gray sky, the imperial brightness of the buildings, and the eternal snow on the ground. With a singular taste for enormity, all the classical marvels of architecture have been reproduced, and I visit exhibitions of painting in premises twenty times as vast as Hampton Court. What painting! A Norwegian Nebuchadnezzar built the stairways of the government buildings; even the subordinates I saw were already prouder than Brahmas, and I trembled at the aspect of the guardians of colossi and the building supervisors. By grouping the buildings around squares, courts and enclosed terraces, they have ousted the cabbies. The parks present primitive nature cultivated with superb art, there are parts of the upper town that are inexplicable: an arm of the sea, without boats, rolls its sleet-blue waters between quays covered with giant candelabra. A short bridge leads to a postern directly under the dome of the Sainte-Chapelle. This dome is an artistic structure of steel about fifteen thousand feet in diameter.
>
> From certain points on the copper footbridges, on the platforms, on the stairways that wind around the markets and the pillars, I thought I might form an idea of the depth of the city! This is the prodigy I was unable to discover: what are the levels of the other districts below and above the acropolis? For the stranger of our day exploration is impossible. The business district is a circus in a uniform style with arcaded galleries.[18]

So where are we here? What is this all about? It is not essential for us to know whether he is describing London or Stockholm, where he also went, or whether he went farther to Norway, or if he is bringing up his memories of Paris, or again whether he is in the throws of a bit too much hashish (a possibility that cannot be excluded either). Simply, at that moment, it is what he wanted to write. And it was not in the least acceptable by his time's vision, its discourse, its architecture, and its rulers. That is what made him give up and go live elsewhere. It is what is left for us.

There is a moment that is either too soon or too late as the time within which the event could have been realized is passed. This is why it makes me happy to be able to talk to you now.

I found that the histories of Age III of the city immediately call up a reference to their inspiration in Rimbaud's texts. So why must it have taken all this time for it to reach the architect?

It didn't happen through words. It happened because you were telling me earlier that you "were carrying acuity in a train," then you began to doodle, then to draw pillars, and then, little by little the Cité de la Musique appeared in your drawings, and now it will exist in a city. This strange construction came to you through one experience—I don't know if it was painful—perhaps an acuteness that is taut. In any case, it is a physical experience that you describe.

As to poetry, what was it that was excluded as poetry, as poetry of architecture? And by whom and why?

What is it that they are trying to do to humankind when they prevent it from inhabiting poetry in architecture? Clearly, they are not interested in its well-being.

C.d.P. I was struck, not too long ago, by a letter in the correspondence between Goethe and Schiller. Goethe writes (I am citing from memory): "Yesterday, I went to the opera; the sets were marvelous. Ah! theatrical architecture is exhilarating, it's great! It has to obey all the rules of architecture, but in addition it must be enchanting, light, varied."

And strangely, he adds: "But this is not the case for architecture itself."[19] This is particularly not what is demanded of architecture. It is asked to express "seriousness and rigidity." Architecture is that which is serious; it is authority and inflexible law. In other words, everyone must know that power is present, that life is harsh.

P.S. Goethe wrote a horrible sentence: "I prefer injustice to disorder."

C.d.P. So in the theater, the opera, the decorators could go all the way; they were allowed to enchant. But in the midst of this, the nineteenth century is already making its first appearance and it is exit time for the Age of Enlightenment. In this letter, Goethe assigns a function to architecture. His vision is that of the time, and it was destined to have a great future. I don't think that we have gotten out of it yet. Architecture and the city express society as it is. They form a whole with its own conflicts. We always find in it, on the one hand, order, money, and power and, on the other, the screen, the simulacra, and special effects. This has been the sole dominant vision for far too long. The systematic and essential function of architecture and urbanism were thought to be that of expressing order, and thus boredom lurked somewhere in it as well. As Bataille put it, architecture is charged with imposing "a mathematical frock coat," along with the taste for authority and a yoke on a world that really preferred life. Bataille viewed architecture as a prison. If we look at a Brazilian slum, a *favela*—though it is true that the people are poor, and there is now the terror of crime, so I wouldn't want to romanticize it—there is a vitality in these neighborhoods; there is invention in the organization and grouping of these constructions of cinder blocks and corrugated steel perched on impossible hills facing the ocean, each unique, each reflecting an individual history that is very exciting, that is life itself. This is building against order.

And how could this exist in the administered world that is ours? The world in which the living must pass through the logos of the administeree. It is hard to escape from this but we are trying. And there are sometimes escape hatches, new possibilities, because politics no longer seeks to impose an order through architecture. Politicians often seek to ward off the inhabitants' displeasure. And also, the new law, the law of the erratic and blind order, is money. Sometimes one can fool it.

Archigram was ready: let's divert, literally and ironically

seize all the freedoms that technique is promising us—it is a wonderful and playful world. We could perhaps make Rimbaud's *Villes,* bit by bit, accidentally, that is, if we can speak in terms of equivalences. But generally speaking, the world isn't made this way; we have only a weak grasp on it. When we look at how it is evolving, it becomes an enormous accumulation of products, of objects. A colossal pile of junk. That is what we are facing. After the postwar period, the period of urban expansion, when we entered the period that could be called postgrowth, when population growth became stable, a new time began. Previously, there had been a great deal of construction to deal with a deep crisis. Never in history had there been so much construction done so rapidly. The size of urban areas increased tenfold on the basis of uncertain and experimental doctrines. Suddenly, there are fewer children, and probably already too many schools in Europe, or it seems that way. Will it be necessary to destroy them or put them to other uses? What are we going to do with them? The issue is now not so much building new. We are entering a time when we will constantly transfigure and transform the world instead of founding it. It is an aspect of this new time that I call the Age III of the city. As soon as population growth slowed down, we entered this time of modification. I'm not the only one to talk about it. Examples among many are the Lyon Opera by Jean Nouvel, the remodeling of the Fresnoy by Bernard Tschumi, or what I myself did on Rue Nationale on rows of dwellings from the sixties. This has become quite striking at present. We are using the existent and its major structures as a first project, a basic narrative, that we then transform, reveal, separate, or preserve because there is no longer anything anywhere that is naked or untouched. But this calls for no less creativity. It often demands much more creativity: since there is no longer a shared and universal code, we have to invent each time. It is a return to a geography, a history, to time finally given its due, reinterpreted. And this beginning narrative could just as well be a classical city as postwar urban areas and their vast expanses, this world so hurriedly built. We have to acknowledge that our elders were very efficient. Until 1963, 1964, millions of people were homeless, and there were *bidonvilles*[20] all around Paris. In twenty years, there was more construction than in the previous two thousand years. Fifty percent of the French population lived during this Age II; that's a lot. By using industrial methods and thinking, they were able, in some twenty years, to give a roof to everyone. It was a true big bang, a shock, at times an almost catastrophic expansion. Could we know if it would have been possible to proceed differently? That would be another discussion. It is done. The die is cast.

Now that this evolution has slowed down, we find ourselves in a difficult world in which recent and ancient constructions surround us. Will there yet be a new Rimbaud to imagine the layers below and above the Acropolis? Is imagination enough?

In Europe, we are seeing and living in this recent and ancient patrimony, this city with its two contradictory ages, this bigger city that has spread out. When there is no longer need to expand, to dream of another future in another place, we become anxious. But there will always be the need to transform, because that which was done in the past is now so often intolerable. This is why the new program is to reenchant bit by bit, to reinvent those places that were not successful, that didn't succeed in bringing us something. This involves leaving the architecture that spoke only of order and power. But there must be the will and money.

P.S. You used the word "transformation" a lot. I'm thinking of Rimbaud. He speaks of linkages, of footbridges, of bridges, that begin the process of connecting the most dissimilar things, things we don't expect to see together because they have been produced, he writes, during epochs of superstitions. And henceforth, these things offer themselves to his vision as entirely linked even though they were never expected to be together. And this seems to me to be a very impressive moment in the history of metaphysics. This Western metaphysics comes to an end with major devastations at the edge of a hole. If there was so much building done in twenty years' time, it is because there had been so much destruction. The word "transformation" leads us directly into a digression, as I would like to cite a book by François Julien, *Traité d'efficacité*.[21] He writes that the Chinese think architecture differently. Even though the impact of the West, particularly of the Soviet Union, can be felt in the weight and violence of its architecture, the key theme for China is indeed transformation.

C.d.P. In our cities that have to be transformed, history appears in either simplified or unreadable form, or again masked by the superposition of contradictory epochs and doctrines. For centuries, there was a very progressive expansion of urban areas, with some sudden efforts of planned transformation and beautification. And then the thread suddenly broke. Just like rivers that flood, towns too can overflow their banks. In the middle of the last century there was a belief in the advent of a world that would be completely controlled, that could be separated from contingency, from innumerable individual cases, from the very notion of place. The project gives the impression that the goal was to establish a universal grid over the whole of the planet in the same gesture at play in the past in cartography and in the discovery and conquest of the planet. The technical logos, the vector of progress, was at work. It analyzed; it made it possible to think in terms of numbers, to create series, models. I recently read Le Corbusier's substantial volume *La ville radieuse*.[22] All of this somewhat heavy literature sings the praise of the new effectiveness. Everything is solved. The world no longer contains unknowns or any rough spots. The same buildings are planned for Oslo and Rio. It is a paradise of norms and typical objects. After the war, as if it were a pacifying balm, it is the very ideal of universalism of the West that is realized in this planetary urban project. That is why this is called International style, one belonging to a time of reconciliation and the cold war as well as a time of planning. Later on, this now victorious universal came to be known as globalization. So the universal is no longer achieved in urbanism, no longer in what Le Corbusier called "human settlements" but in the economy.

As you say, this globalization is seen in China. In the West, the references to these modern metamorphoses have been industrialism, Fordism, and also the trigger of the eradicating principle of the October Revolution in Russia. In China we have witnessed another side of the modern universalist project, Maoism. I remember a brigade of Chinese architects who came to see me: "We would like to ask you about your ideas." The year was 1980. So I talked about architecture. One of them says: "It's interesting, because back home in China, there were never any architects. That's a bourgeois invention. What we had were masons."

"So how was the Forbidden City built? With shots of rice wine?"

"They were masons, not architects!"

"There must have been a plan? In France, we have a tradition that also came out of the mason trade. Phillibert Delorme used to say, 'an architect is a mason who speaks Latin.' There were of course masons who were inspired and learned, who did draw plans.

"No, it's a bourgeois notion. In China, we have plain masons."

So I adopt the same tone as the Chinese: "Yes, there was a time when we too thought it was not good for the people that a single person would be in charge of everyone's happiness; we too believed that everyone had to participate in the design and realization of dwellings, so we worked collectively in groups, but we found we were wrong."

Then they gave me interesting details: "You know, back home, since there are no architects, we organize teams. One team draws up the plans, another draws the walls, another the roofs, and then all of these plans are sent out to the countryside and there, there are groups we call 'planning brigades' who come up with the final plans. No one can say that he/she is the author of the building—so this is real popular democracy." What they described is a hybrid version of Taylorism and equalitarianism, always along with the idea of universalizing. They wanted to be sure that no one, ever, could claim to create, that there would no longer be any author, that the society that produces secretes this machine world that formats human beings, that itself would be a machine.

These two dreams of technical control, that of modern urbanism and that of communism, are broken. Real life has been elsewhere. In both cases, living together in a different way but based on technology has not worked. And after the great efforts of the universal ideal of state planning, the city entered the realms of confusion, profusion, and diffusion. Today, we are facing a city that is at times extraordinary and at others nothing. It is fragmented, dispersed, in some places tragic, blocked in some others, and in other places very exciting. This is the advent of another time where, in spite of science, the shattering of dreams of planning and the prospect of a nondomesticated future has generated a fear of the future, a fear of even minimal risk. Who would have thought that the futuristic visions and drawings of the 1920s and 1930s, in which everything was bigger, straighter, and more enormous, would lead to the chaos we experience today?

The whole of the idea of the universal generated by the logos is now shattering on the individual case, the makeshift, on a contingent that is perhaps specific to our topos. Each site is a microcosm, a fragment of an old village with three HLM,[23] a controversy over a freeway, and someone who refuses to sell her house. Each time, it is a scene that is never the same, and we have to requestion our tools and begin anew. I feel that this is almost a trick history plays on us. It is as if place took its revenge through the return of unique cases. These, again, require us to think in terms of the accidental in order to build, to make the city, this by working in situ, case by case, sometimes with makeshift means. No one could have foreseen this thirty years ago.

P.S. You are saying: "I've always loved horizons, ridgelines, cutouts in the sky." And also: "Horizons are paradises. Look as far as possible. Numbers and signs swap courses. 'The cuckoo sings where one is not,' reads a Haiku poem. Poles were sometimes set against the background, and the sky brought closer in, palpable, a wall surface before which a number of objects converse."

And this interests me very much: "At a distance, oftentimes in the background, there is a deep forest and its edge in the almost disturbing shadowy darkness, a series of trees behind a geometrical framework."

So you speak about your drawings, and this leads you to wonder about the nature of an anti-nature form, like that of the earliest things. Are you improvising there?

C.d.P. The drawings, yes. Daniel Rivière, for his book *Généalogies des Formes,* asked me about these drawings; they are commentaries.

P.S. You say: "As we face a landscape, we are always in a state of astonishment, of wonder, illumination, epiphany. A radical, primordial astonishment as we face the presence of things. Our existence is then given to us once again, mysterious, incomprehensible. This experience, at times fueled by unaccustomed, extreme conditions, is that of architectural emotion and of the ideas it stirs. Upon our return, going out the next morning, the world strikes us as a great enterprise, industrious, talkative, and blind, a gigantic lie. We want to recover the enchantment; we remember the evidence, the obviousness of it, but must ever seek the keys to it once again."[24]

What is this "architectural emotion?"

C.d.P. There is something at play between the body, space, sensations, and time. I often call this the "presence effect" in contrast to the "signification effect." There is strong evidence for this. Sometimes, I think of dreams whose keys are lost. We know there is something, we retain some clues, but then we didn't note them, or it is the next day. I don't know—the key has been lost. It seems to me that if there is no astonishment in the face of sometimes simple, already seen things, in the face of ugliness and beauty, then I think there are no ideas.

P.S. "A radical, primordial astonishment."[25]

C.d.P. Of course, this astonishment is revitalized in powerful places. I remember this happening in Teotihuacán, Mexico, when I first saw the site. In that landscape surrounded by fairly even mountain peaks, the pyramids took on the appearance of a human challenge to nature, an attempt to equal and even best it. The analogy between the form of the pyramids and that of the mountains is immediately evident, except that the pyramids are more beautiful. They are perfect while the mountains seem to be impure attempts made by slightly fumbling gods. And it is astonishing, since this civilization rose in complete ignorance of what existed in Egypt. In spite of this, there is a same use of schemes, I wouldn't say concepts, but the spatial schemes are the same. There is a general axis as well as structured court-yards and ordered empty spaces. And then there are buildings and pyramids with square bases: the marks of human beings' radical astonishment about the planet and the whys of it. From where did it come? What is it? Who gave it all of these forms, this life? Thus, who are we? It is the same question. And there, these answers are the beginning of architecture. It is not just building in order to shelter but also to be. It is the enterprise of another nature, an enigma responding to another enigma.

How do you react to this idea? As for me, I remain awed. It is not just an archaeological site, or at least it is speaking to me as if it were day one. It makes us experience the otherness of the received world as it reveals us to ourselves. These pyramids, they are a way of creating an alternative world proving man-kind to itself, founding this world as such and ripping it away from nature. Otherwise, what are we?

It is not written; that wouldn't have been enough. It had to be built with enormous effort to make it indestructible. They have yet to bring to light the 90 percent of it that is still buried in the sand. In Mexico City, not far from there, when the Spanish first got there, they were so impressed that they too made an enormous effort to wipe out the pyramid. Mexico City was a

Venice, a city of canals, which the Spanish filled up. There were plans but they disappeared into silence, censorship. For a long time, nothing was divulged, and only recently, during the 1930s, this gigantic pyramid that had existed in the middle of Mexico City was discovered and is in the process of being excavated. The Spanish saw it as something that threatened who they were. But destroying the Aztecs was not an easy task. It all had to be leveled, and they had to claim that this civilization, this architecture, had never existed.

P.S. I am intrigued by the notion of a *radical, primordial astonishment* and by your locating it over there. One could place it in Egypt or wherever you want. I would bring it right here, the *radical, primordial astonishment* in the face of the most familiar, everyday events such as your gesture of pouring this glass of water.

There is a book, Jean-Paul Sartre's *Nausea,* set just before World War II. *Nausea* is a great book. Everything is stifling. It describes a blocked situation. In the nineteenth century, it is as if history were not progressing. Everyone is repeating the same things. Sartre even uses Balzac's *Eugénie Grandet* to show the extent to which conversations had fallen into ridiculous repetition. And in the famous scene in the park, you remember the passage where suddenly the root of a tree triggers the revelation of nothingness. Later on, Sartre was to deprive himself of this radical astonishment. He became frightened of it. He became an adherent; he didn't trust his revelation. It is something very heavy to carry. If you carry *acuteness* or your everyday radical astonishment, that is good. But one can fall asleep and say: "I'll remember my radical astonishment some other day."

C.d.P. Making the choice at a given moment to attempt building instead of dreaming in some way means learning to convert one's radical astonishment. Thinking of a project means waking this astonishment up. Building, seeing the construction appear, also brings about this awakening. But building is not only positive. My profession has forced me to maintain a steadying and everyday contact with reality and kept me from drifting away. But there is a danger because one must go to meetings, the price must be right, and this might quickly chase the dream away and lock astonishment in the closet. In those cases, effort doesn't pay.

P.S. What is it that you are attached to in a building? What is it that you put in it that is a message between you and yourself?

C.d.P. There are a certain number of obsessions that keep coming back, that make their own way, that become work instruments that others end up adopting. But at the start, it is not good to be too attached to a prethought thing. I like this image of messages between myself and myself. The site, the project itself offers suggestions. And then, there are some traits that come to the fore, that come up often without being consciously called up, themes that I have already worked on. For instance, for the elliptical hall of the Cité de la Musique, I worked a lot with Pierre Boulez. He repeatedly asked me: "Don't you want it to be rectangular?" And I answered: "No." It is elliptical. In fact, the ellipse is very bad for acoustic. It creates fixed points; it is very risky. There are no elliptical concert halls. The focalizations of sound are the worst in them. Moreover, I wanted this hall to be high, about fifty feet; thus the ceilings could not be used for the first reflections of sound. During a big meeting, Pierre Boulez asked me one last time if I would consider making it a parallelepiped. I again said no, it has to be elliptical. So he answered: "I don't understand the form, but I understand the will to a form. It is the same in music; if there is no will to a form, one doesn't go anywhere. So, now, let's go, let's follow the ellipse!" And with Xu Ya Ying, the acoustician, we found many other means to make the ellipse work very well for the sound. So a moment in making a plan can yield some things to which one becomes attached.

P.S. And why did you want an ellipse?

C.d.P. You provided the answer yourself on the day we went to see it. You said: "I understand very well, I used to suffer from asthma." I explained to you that in concert halls I found it awful to feel frozen in place while the music made me think of free motion. The ellipse introduces a space in which limits are not discontinuous. The disappearance of boundary markers was something I really wanted. From various positions, the hall appears to be big or intimate. And then I pierced the walls; I installed boxes high up, for the public and also for light and acoustic. There is a feeling that there are other things behind these boxes, a populated exterior that could open up. And you answered me: "I used to suffer from asthma; I understand opening up very well."

At that moment I remembered that I had had asthma until age five. And this might perhaps be the reason that I am always driven to break down compact masses. I feel I want to know how to open up space in order to define a place. Something must cross it. This movement is the message coming back.

I don't know if the asthma sufferer is anguished by total fluidity—at least he is breathing—but he must be even more anxious in closed, too tight spaces. What I mean by this is that we think with our bodies when we practice architecture.

P.S. The same when we write.

C.d.P. I was saying that perceiving is already thinking. Architects have to give form to the knowledge their own bodies have and turn it into a working tool, as well as share it with others. Thus they should think about the way we perceive and of what we can perceive. We perceive with our feet, our ears, our eyes, with smells, rhythms, whispers, and the brain.

And this invites us to move or not to move; it fixes us at one point or it petrifies us—movement of the body and of thought.

Like many others I was reading Rimbaud before thinking in terms of architecture. I have in front of me the letter called "The Seer's Letter" that Rimbaud wrote to his friend Paul Demeny on 15 May 1871: "Romanticism has never been fairly appraised; who would have? Critics! The romantics, who so clearly prove that the song is infrequently the work of a singer, which is to say rarely is its thought both sung and *understood* by the singer."[26]

And the famous phrase: "For I is someone else. If the brass awakes as horn, it can't be to blame. This much is clear: I'm around for the hatching of my thought; I watch it, I listen to it; I release a stroke from the bow; the symphony makes its rumblings in the depths or leaps fully formed onto the stage. If old fools hadn't completely misunderstood the nature of the [self], We wouldn't be constantly sweeping up these millions of skeletons that, since time immemorial, have hoarded products of their monocular intellects, a blindness of which they claim authorship!"[27]

And further down, he writes: "I mean that you have to be a *seer,* mold oneself into a *seer.* The Poet makes himself into a *seer* by a long, involved, and logical *derangement of all the senses.*"[28]

We could say that, even though these words did not introduce Cézanne who was on the margins, elsewhere, they truly did introduce Picasso, Pollock, De Kooning, Rothko. I am making this passage toward painting—toward a post-Rimbaud.

P.S. The whole of the poetry of the century is marked by Rimbaud. He is a moment of incandescence. A moment we need to take literally and in all its meanings.

When I worked on Picasso, I was surprised when I found out that he was reading *A Season in Hell* at the time he was painting *Les Demoiselles d'Avignon* in 1906, 1907, which is totally strange.

The relationship is not at all evident. But here it is: Picasso was always in touch with poets. When he was dying, he quoted Apollinaire; he remembered the Apollinaire of Max Jacob's time. For painting, poetry is an old story. Picasso surely had a strong sense of poetry. It is true that at one point he was writing constantly; the result was *Picasso's Writings* in Spanish. Picasso's paintings should also be listened to in Spanish; otherwise one can't understand them. And one also needs to see what he tried to capture in his writings that are not successful poems but angry experiments. There are screaming notations without punctuation, particularly when he experienced difficulties with his painting. One has to hear them with their Spanish rhythm. The eye listens, as someone has put it. It is something that happened a lot in France, this relationship between poetry and painting. So it is very enlightening that architecture is linked to a vision of painting. Why is there this constant exchange between painters and poets? Mallarmé and Manet, Claudel and Dutch painting, Artaud and Van Gogh. Instead of looking at a Van Gogh painting as if we were sleepwalking, we can only see it if we have in mind—and thus it's very difficult—Artaud's text *Le suicidé de la société*. There is Breton, Aragon with uneven successes, and even Diderot, Baudelaire, Delacroix; it is constant. Why has there been this reciprocal porousness between painters and writers? It is as if it were the same physical struggle. I believe that from there it is not difficult to also go to music, and specifically, we should not cut the language of vision. Musical vision, that is what Rimbaud means. A thought hooking into another and pulling it. Why do people deprive themselves from perceiving? That is the great question. Have they been forbidden to do so? Or do they find safety in the prohibition?

3. The Power of Dreams

P.S. The tower you built for LVMH[1] seemed to me like an eruption of desire in New York.

C.d.P. Many New Yorkers have asked me: "How could you have imagined this tower? How did you do it? Why haven't others done it?" I answered that I first sacrificed several square feet of empty space on each floor and requested the right to not align the whole of the facade on the street. At the outset, everyone believed that this would be against the zoning code. But when I asked if we could build setbacks and bends in the facades, the specialized consultant replied, "Why not"? Complex calculations were required to find the possible ratio of concaveness that was possible. And I found out very subtle regulations in a text that had to be based on tradeoffs: you give up some volume here; you have to take it back elsewhere. This "mercantile" rule utterly lacks preconceived notions regarding "style." This is very interesting. In Paris, it is impossible to play with setbacks and bulges in facades. Regulations for lining up the facades are very strict; protrusions and hollows are regulated according to rules issued from classical architecture.

In this New York project I sought to avoid reproducing the

staircaselike line typical of the silhouette of New York's buildings. I wanted to go beyond this line in order to create a direct, strong verticality and thus give the tower the greater presence that had been implicitly requested when they called it a flagship building. The consultant, Michael Parley, answered me: "You are not required to build up the alignment as on setbacks gradually diminishing to form an arrow type of line. You are required to make a building that would have a presence on this line, that is, one point of contact can be sufficient." I found this unbelievable! There is a freedom in the texts of the regulations that is very little used, and probably little known, because it is often unthinkable or irrational in New York to not fully use the square feet available on each level, to not fully use each story even though these square feet can be regained by building higher. In contrast, what is well known is the right to build more surface if one provides some extra public space on the ground floor. But the basic economic reasoning leads to being blind to the other freedoms granted by the regulations. It is a dense, complex text that only some initiates are able to interpret, and moreover only if the question is asked. Then the text grants or refuses the authorization through the voice of an exegete who has to take his time and in turn consult others. And it is this text, amended, modified once or twice per century, that has framed the volumetry of Manhattan—the relationship between mass and empty space—and has given the streets their gothic proportion and their light.

P.S. I would like to go back to something you told me during our last meeting, namely, that we can think without language, that we could "architecturize" ourselves outside of language.

C.d.P. It is as if we had two ways of thinking, two parallel conceptions. It is true, language is always present. For instance, there is the text of the regulation or of the project, and then the ideas with which I am challenging it. So can we think without language? I am constantly asking myself how the work of think-

ing in the visible, in space, is happening. A number of painters told us how it works, among them Matisse, Picasso, Klee,
Kandinsky. But when reading them we become aware that they
are using words to explain what they have done after the fact,
that they first thought with lines, contours, images, masses.
They obviously did not use words while they were creating
their art. I would even say that it is because they were not able to
verbalize their work that they were able to think them through
other means. I mentioned what seems to me to be our Western
prejudice, that the idea of any intelligence is a process that presupposes abstraction, formula, and concept. This discrimination
began with rational thought in ancient Greece. To think presupposes being able to extract oneself from the infinite magma of
sensations by which we are enveloped. It means being able to
abstract experience so as to universalize it; it involves designating, naming, finding the formula that will allow the thinker to
bypass sensible experience. Things are no longer felt. We or others come to an understanding of a given thing, and then all of
this work is turned into a repertory. The memory of the event,
of the architecture, of the emotion is stored through language.
There is an accumulation of other people's knowledge, of that of
humankind, which seems to be entirely contained in formulas.
Like money, there is a virtual equivalent at the table, at the pic-
nic, at making, and at rejoicing.

Since then, all of the progress of intelligence appears like a
march always on the way toward more abstraction, always resolving the particular in the universal. This process triumphs
today with the computer, the memory machine that can calculate to infinity, that appears as a superior stage of thinking
performance.

And when this language is challenged, that is when there is
an opportunity for poetry to make its appearance. That is why
writing, literature, is vital. My work progressed when I came
back to the truth of lived experience. We need to feel and feel
again. This is because you have to learn to act according to sensations and to manipulate them. When working on a project, my

impressions become figures, schemes that are not language. At the same time, we also have to calculate and understand, listen and read. We have to see and talk, listen and read all at once. We have to sort out what can be explained and what cannot. Speak afterward or almost at the same time. Listening, seeing.

P.S. Can I ask you, if you happen to dream of architecture, do you dream that you are walking around in one of your constructions?

C.d.P. Yes. For instance, I dreamed of the first building that I built, a water tower, but without being aware of it. I remember that the dream happened in a forest, at night; there was fire and a celebration. The people were worried about the coming daybreak that would mark the end of the party. A tower appears, lit by the fire; it has ten sides, and on each side in a loggia there is someone I know.

The weird thing is that it is a set of circumstances, chance, accident, and probably my own will that led me to build this tower shortly after, without thinking for a moment about the dream. Long after, as I was sorting papers I found the text I had scribbled on the morning after awakening from this dream. I remember it well.[2]

It is only with hindsight that the rediscovery of this dream of the tower that I actually built later on became superimposed with this premonition.

Sometimes I dream I am discovering colors that do not exist. I am entranced. I have the impression that I have the gift of inventing new colors, pastels that do not exist. I have the sensation of being freed by colors.

One of my projects, for a tower in Japan that ended up not being built, privileged the idea of light and color. The building was supposed to be only a support that had to reflect an ever-changing electric light that could be controlled. I had experimented in a smaller way in the concert hall I built, the Cité de la Musique, with acoustical window nooks in color. In a dream, the hall became enormous.

P.S. I think again about this facade. It seems that you have said that it is not a facade but a body, whence it triggers a strong impression that the elements are pinned together, that you succeeded in creating hollows where in principle this wasn't planned. In spite of the preliminary lining up and equalization of space, you have managed to create hollows. I was thinking, as I was listening to you, about this Fragonard painting that could be likened to something that is thought and is thinkable in Chinese. It was the moment when the two civilizations met before the time when this probably premature dialogue was scuttled. The great discovery of the Baroque and the sudden appearance of China as a horizon suitable for questioning are two events contemporary to each other. We'll discuss these some more because they have to do with hollows, with diagonals, and with other ways of experiencing space before calculation comes into play. There is something here that seems to me to be very important. In "the place and the formula *[le lieu et la formule]*," as Rimbaud puts it, we hear formula and not place. I asked you about the places of your memory because the destruction of a place that has enchanted one's childhood is a major trauma. I experienced two such places in my life that were destroyed, wiped out. The first one was a house destroyed by the Germans in 1942 on Ré Island. It stood in the way of their firing line. This forces me to dream of this place to the extent that it has disappeared. Recently a storm destroyed the facade of this same rebuilt house. The cyclone that came over the French coasts redestroyed the facade, forcing me to redream it, the dream being at that moment a work of repair of the place itself, a dream that understands me to be an integral part of the existence of the place.

My second experience happened around Bordeaux, in a place where houses and gardens have been destroyed and replaced by a mall. This destruction is forcing me to keep reconstructing the place with a tiring precision, to dream the stairways, the hallways, the roofs, and to reassure myself that they couldn't all have disappeared. Unfortunately this never works. *To have been* is very different from *having been destroyed* because the *having been* persists. We inhabit the *having been* in a form of persistent loss. Everything that is built is built on something that is either repressed or destroyed, or on a violent desire to affirm the impossible. It is a relationship with time that is immediately translated into a more or less violent intervention in space. I once had a personal experience in which language suddenly existed by itself. I was writing, and the words began to detach themselves. I had the impression of passing through the mirror and finding myself in a place where language and the world are made of the same substance. This resembles what Proust evokes when he writes that very small things can sometimes suddenly trigger the reciprocal irruption both in the past and the present of two different places. Time then disappears. It is the famous hypothesis of time found again as space.

It is yet different in *Passion fixe*.[3] The narrator feels like putting an end to everything and killing himself. He thus puts himself in a radically negative situation, and then he has an experience of space, of the leveling of space, of the leveling of the text itself. He takes pains to explain that there is no alcohol or drug involved in this feeling, and it is not a hallucination either. The walls seem to be sliding in on themselves. Perspectives appear on the left and on the right. It is not an earthquake. Rather, paradoxically, there is a great sense of serenity.

Silence shone in its orbit. I could see it: a spherical silence.

The narrator very calmly asks himself about his death. Am I dead? And he realizes that it is not that either. This movement continues, going northward, a strange north, not at all terrestrial or celestial, though we could call it a kind of equinox if we were still in a world of compass and orientation.

The thing I find interesting in that experience is that the narrator throws his gun in the Seine. The reason is obvious: killing himself at that moment would be a mistake because he finds himself within a living experience where everything—forms, sounds, colors, smells—is changed and where things stand rough, naked, without contour and background. The narrator stands on the quays along the Seine and he says that he is one of those things. They are not in front of me, he says, nor around me; they are there, freed from any sort of orientation and meaning.

"The right to have no meaning should be the first right of man since the second right to be wished for should be not to be a man."

So what this translates into is that the character is on the bridge. We need to think at length about this idea of bridge or small span.

The bridge is the Pont Neuf swept with an ill Parisian wind. The character has a fever, but his main feeling is that he is pierced through by a transparent column, a stake of certitude. He has the impression that his body is full of surprises; he feels no positive unity but rather nostrils, temples, ears, cheeks.

"Does this belong to me? he asked, surprised. A nose, a forehead, eyes, throat, a city, noises, stones, a bridge, a river, hands, legs, used shoes, breath, a beating heart, blood . . ."

As you see, this experience is an experience of very strong dispossession in which the architectural affirmation brings on this sensation to a certain extent. It is a sensation of being called to be the one to manipulate one's own sensations.

C.d.P. The architect is precisely someone who has had to learn to manipulate his or her sensations, to think them. What has intrigued me from the time I started working is that space and language, the *topos* and the *logos,* the place and the formula, are fields that are rigorously distinct, two parallel environments but with surface contact. They are associated like air and water, they cannot be split apart. It is because of this that I am preoccupied with the notion of thinking without language.

P.S. You mean that without language as a mean of expression, there is a language of place.

C.d.P. The place or the bridge is not a fragment of language but a space, a visible ensemble. It can be perceived. At a given moment, it is for me like a center or a zone differentiated from others that is emitting toward me. This happens as if it were emitting. That is sensible experience. Afterward, it can be given a name. From there, each thing can be isolated, and that is the experience of rational thought: things exist not only when we perceive them, they have an existence on their own, outside of ourselves. The self is not the center. But it has to remain. It must not dissolve. This is a crucial experience that constitutes us.

P.S. Space and language are exactly on an equal footing.

C.d.P. But you said earlier that space is already language.

P.S. No, it is being. Even silence is a sort of language in the deepest sense. Can we think without language? We have to answer with an absolute "yes" if language is a question of verbalized representation as in "I think, therefore I am." Since I is another, we have taken a step outside of the *cogito*. Can we think without representation? Yes, we need to go further on this question of language without representation that is signaling a poetic experience. We have to be very careful with our words: it is not poetry as we mean by a poem but the experience of being.

C.d.P. Yes.

P.S. In order for the sort of event to appear that Heidegger called a *thing*, for it to appear to *us*, we need to realize that this occurs through something very small, minute, very intimate.

C.d.P. When you were talking about the destruction of those places that "forced" you to dream about them, I came to think of a language born from the place. This something so very intimate, this spatial origin, this visible primitive, is the base for the painter's and the poet's work. For Rimbaud, it is vision. He travels again the places that are becoming others. This goes beyond the places of origin. Always before, there was "the place." After Rimbaud, the experience of wonderment is a transmutation. We apprehend that place, space, the visible, is fundamentally irreducible to language.

In the 1960s, the semiotic trend that saw language as a universal matrix helped me understand this but, so to speak, by default. Indeed, this seemed to me to be a stumbling block for architecture precisely because, by denying the specific character of space, by denying its autonomy from language, this trend was not able to grasp architecture.

P.S. It is the power of calculation, of formalism.

C.d.P. Language ceaselessly looking at and thinking language.

P.S. But that is not language. It is reduced language. One of Heidegger's texts comes to mind here. It's called *the Thing (das Ding),* and it fits right into our discussion: "The abolition of all distances has brought the distanceless to dominance. In the default of nearness the thing remains annihilated as a thing in our sense. But when and in what way do things exist as things? This is the question we raise in the midst of the dominance of the distanceless."[4]

I am struck by Heidegger's signal; what is it that remained absent? Smallness, docility, action resembling the thing, and each time small, without appearance. Small is the thing, the span and the plow, the tree and the pond, the stream and the mountain, the heron and the stag, the horse and the bull. "Things, each thinging and each staying in its own way, are mirror and clasp, book and picture, crown and cross."[5]

Heidegger is emphasizing the *modest,* the small; "things are . . . compliant and modest in number, compared with the countless objects everywhere of equal value." To turn language into an object should not be a major concern.

As an architect, you are standing in the midst of the countless spread of objects, all the more so if you are trying to build a thing in a city. There is nothing more difficult than that: "But things are also compliant and modest in number, compared with the countless objects everywhere of equal value, compared with the measureless mass of men as living beings. Men alone, as mortals, by dwelling attain to the world as world. Only what conjoins itself out of world becomes a thing."[6]

In contrast, a Cité de la Musique, or a water tower, or whatever, is born in a modest way. I assume that you are wondering if these are things rather than just some more buildings. The question is to know how we stand within this conclusion of metaphysics and whether we are standing or wobbling.

C.d.P. We need the proximity, the assembling of things, and also movement, the abolition of distances. We need the tiny, but also the enormous, and we need to give a presence to the enormous. The difficulty lies perhaps in the abolition of distances, the ubiquity, the perception of a body that is in several places at once, that can be in motion from one place to another. A body less rooted in proximity than it was sixty years ago, more virtual but nonetheless real. A present mistake of architecture is to think that place doesn't matter, that it no longer has a future. If place no longer exists, we are no longer present, nor are we in motion from one place to another. This is the domination of the "distanceless," the screen.

P.S. Let us look again to Rimbaud's "Vagabonds": "I, hard-pressed to find the place and the formula." It's a violent scene. Verlaine suddenly appears; he is the negative companion. The negative companion reproaches the one who is saying "I" (Rimbaud) that he is not doing what he promised. Because of him, there will be a return to exile and slavery:

> Pitiable brother! What agonizing vigils I owed him! I was not embracing this enterprise fervently. I had made sport of his infirmity.
>
> Through my fault we would return to exile, to slavery. He imagined me a very strange jinx and an innocent, and he supplied disquieting reasons.
>
> I responded by snickering at this Satanic doctor, and finished by getting to the window. I created, beyond the countryside traversed by bands of rare music, phantoms of future nocturnal luxury.
>
> After this vaguely hygienic diversion, I would stretch myself out on a straw mattress. And almost every night,

as soon as I was asleep, the poor brother would rise, his mouth decayed, his eyes torn out,—just as he saw himself in his dreams!—and while howling his illusion of idiotic grief, he'd drag me into the room.

I had, in fact, in all sincerity of spirit, taken the pledge to restore him to his primitive state of son of the sun,—and we would wander, nourished by the wine of the caverns and the biscuit of the road, I hard-pressed to find the place and the formula.[7]

It is amazing to read Rimbaud in the light of place. It shows that he had good reasons to name several of his illuminations "Cities." The following from the poem "After the Flood" should also be carefully reread:

Circuses
in the still dripping big house with glass panes
a door slammed
the child waved his arms, understood by weather vanes
    and cocks on steeples everywhere, under the glit-
    tering downpour.
a piano in the Alps
Mass and first communions were celebrated at the
    hundred thousand altars of the cathedral
Caravans departed
the Hotel Splendide was erected in the chaos of ice and
    of polar night.
foam, roll above the bridge and over the woods . . .[8]

Rimbaud announces an upheaval of place such that he tries to give a direct feeling of it. He has grasped a movement. What is architecture as a ship?

A youthful couple isolates itself on the ark.[9]

Rimbaud had already gone beyond La Défense.[10] The architectural places that have marked me, from Venice to the Forbidden City, always gave me the impression that there was an enormous future in their past while everything that claimed to be futuristic seemed to be terribly out-of-date. I guess that must be an issue for you, asking yourself if you produced something that *opens up* time. That is probably one of the major issues at stake.

C.d.P. The places built by human beings are metaphysical calendars. In Mexico I had a very strong feeling that men had challenged the gods and had won. In all the cities, I experienced places as the time concentrated in them. You mention that buildings, furniture, are spoken about as a temporal referent by a date: "Don't you think this is very thirties?" Constructions and styles all have dates, and this calendar speaks of many unwritten things. It seems that we express our inexpressible anguish about time through architecture. And all our relationships with time can be expressed through it. Should we "futurize" it? Should we freeze things for the future or leave behind the incomplete? We suffer from a constant temporal problem of transmission, of transformation, of interpretation of this immutable time that is nonetheless moving on. There is nothing we are able to say about it. The only thing that we can do is inscribe it in space. And we have a problem with legacy: do we reject it or not? While I was in Berlin in 1965 I remember paying a visit to Frei Otto, a great engineer who had conceived a project that would cover the port city of Bremen with an immense artificial climate structure. He was a visionary. His house was a modern house without anything striking, no special quality. Simply, a certain number of openings and windows were translucid, made of sanded glass. Frei Otto explained that he thus avoided seeing all the houses with roofs because he couldn't stand seeing the traces of the past. His radical stance was a bit comical. And yet, this isn't a laughing matter; it has actually been our modern ideal since the 1920s, when the grotesque took hold. Architects were locked up in a total, absurd vision. Around this time, in the midsixties, I saw Godard's and Antonioni's films in Paris and in Milan, and their modernity was real, alive, made of the conjunction of historical centers and modern peripheries, and these two filmmakers relished it. They had no beef with the past, no hatred, no doctrine. This in spite of the fact that at that very moment the whole of urbanism was aimed toward a city that would finally and unambiguously be modern—once and for all. Thence it would be without a future. This is striking, for instance, in Brasília. The future had not been included in the city because it was to be designed once and for all. The time of the modern is a time completed, devoid of future. This came to me in 1965 in front of a translucent window.

4. Passion fixe

C.d.P. I would like to draw from your work to talk about form. In your novel *Passion fixe,* for instance, I like the inextricable mixture of the whole.[1] The form leans toward the labyrinth or the kaleidoscope: superposition, intricacies, returns. You compare this text to a cubist composition. I like the dawns, the women, the ads, the Chinese poems; the political, philosophical, erotic, and sarcastic moments. There are moments for everything. I think that this novel contains a way to get rid of the linearity of the text. I almost wanted to call it a "manual" rather than a "novel." Themes mingle with each other. We could list twelve or thirteen themes that keep coming back like a braid, the tones superimposed on each other, the tones of an intimate life for two, of literary history, of politics, of narratives, of philosophy, of China, of solitude, etc. Monologue and conversation, music and making love are expressed in a unique manner. In this fragmentation, different Sollerses follow each other and come together. The experimental Sollers of the 1960s and 1970s, then the one of *Femmes*[2] and of *Paradis,*[3] or again the essayist, the novelist, and the musician. Jazz, rhythm in the sentence—that's your great talent. There is speed, freedom, improvisation.

To be able to preserve an identity even while traversing and borrowing multiple forms is what seems to me the best, the most alive. That is what Wright, Stravinsky, and Picasso achieved, in contrast to Rothko and Pollock, who found and then lost themselves in a formula that was perfect for them but final—a formula into which they were locked. Fixation on the formula, on an absolute signature, is a recurring figure of modern art. Thus, as I read *Passion fixe,* I asked myself about the form and the unity. In your novel, with the multiplicity of the islands traversed, splintering itself takes on a literary form. This splintering is moreover the form of our world, our lives, our cities: telecommunications, ubiquity, fast travel, coded messages, multiple media—fragmented instants, fragmentation and frustration. And each time, the art, the motor of your characters, leads them to protect themselves from this, to "get out of the film." This is why I am thinking of the word "manual." The text awakens in me the desire to set it in various typographies and formats, etc. To eliminate the obligatory linearity, the typographical unity that sticks to the writing. *Passion fixe* explodes in my hands; it is a book I don't necessarily want to read in the numerical order of the pages; rather, I want to read it like the *I Ching,* which makes its appearance often in it and which the characters are consulting. The form of *Passion fixe* is burst, but visually everything appears normal and seems to be a narrative, an organic continuity. You will tell me that this is how life is; it too doesn't have a dominant form. This is precisely why I am thinking of the present-day city. Are you interested in this question of the *overall form*? I am thinking this in the musical sense, that is, in the sense of the perception of the whole of the construction, of the unity. Pierre Boulez told me at the end of our long discussion about the ellipse of the Villette concert hall, the Cité de la Musique, of which we spoke earlier, that if there is no will to a form, there is no longer anything.

P.S. This might be because the form is still too much issued from a will. The less will is involved, the more the question of the form can be asked in another way. Too much will evidences a desire to finish even before beginning. The problem for me is to begin. After, I'll see. What you said seems to be going toward the impression of some sort of freedom. I am attached to this word "novel." Even if it is only a question of polemic, it is necessary in relation to all that is presented as such on the literary market and on the markets of internal life, beginning with the family novel that still clouds human beings, contrary to what one would believe. It is all too easy to verify their statements, their conversations, their reflections, their imagination; they will never be anything beyond the repetition of their familial novel. The familial novel involves a general extension of the social novel, which is only a large instrumentalization of the bond keeping the human being biological. Society is increasingly like an immense family, an immense family that is more and more provincial. This might seem paradoxical in that it might appear that all the value given to the bond of the family novel has exploded, has been destroyed, and that finally there are wanderers free from all ties in search of their identity. But when observing and carefully listening, we always end up with the reiteration of the familial novel. I wanted to briefly discuss the Freudian aspect of the issue. Yes, a form is needed, but on the condition that it not be drawn from a preliminary will or through a repetitive hardening. At present, we are witnessing the fabrication of novelistic replaceable human beings vulnerable to eviction. At the same time, we are witnessing a blocking of fluid, contrasted, and dramatic verbalization. On the one hand we have a static rumination, and on the other a gigantic hemorrhage of superfluity.

C.d.P. You mean that is what we are seeing, that is what is being published.

P.S. That is what is being written, that is what is being lived. Me, I am interested in *disengagement*. How? Almost always through the contestation of the unlivable. Through the desire of being done with the finite. Gradually, the narrative will construct a situation that will be increasingly breathable, comfortable, that will lead us here and there in cities, travels, retreats. The nature of time is changing and thence that of space as well. A big month or a tiny one, a big day or a little day stand the same way as millennia. The relationship with time having changed, the situation of the person who has started to tell something, thus to live in function of that which he or she is telling, that situation will involve organizing a game, something that will be played out. The new identity, far from being in distress, becomes a scanner, which is what I call an MRI: multiple "real close" identities. This is the opposite of the idea of grasping, of taking possession of one or another fixed identity. The title *Passion fixe* is indicative of this contradiction.

C.d.P. I am struck when you say, "I begin by noting the unbelievable." Writing sets up a field of livable magnetization. In this regard, my successful architectural projects always were born of two moments. In a first moment, I notice a thing that is unlivable. This is because the project is either impossible or there is a feeling of incompatibility, of suffocation, even of agoraphobia. But at this stage I still don't know what is the crucial issue that I need to solve. For instance, the town of Grasse is on a steep slope. A courthouse needed to be built in an unstable, slanted, wasted place. This is paradoxical because this building should be stable, visible, well proportioned. Second moment: an idea appears that can transform the unlivable into the livable. This is the idea of a fulcrum point at the center of the rotating movement that exists in that place. Then another idea follows. And the paradox of the beginning has become, is becoming, clarified. The work starts from that point.

P.S. It is not only that something is not livable, but everything is organized so that freedom cannot be, that is, the freedom of an individual wondering what he or she is doing here. A genuine will is at play to offer relativity, anguish, and terror to the individual as if to a child. It is infantilization based on the desire for death. The Program states that it will allow you to live but only to the extent required to make your exit without having wandered too much out of the framework that it has provided for you, this in order for you to be counted. And if you happen to have a talent, a creative libido, an ability to decide, to mold, then the Program will tell you what you can write, paint, or build, while poetry thenceforth becomes the lowest category, which, as everyone knows, is doomed to a miserable marginality. You are now and then probably experiencing this weight, the very opposite of grace, the weight of the moribund program that also occasionally has to produce works, concert halls, dwellings, books. But there is the deep feeling that it is no longer genuine. We are making things that can survive; they are more livable than the unlivable, but barely so.

C.d.P. You are telling us how you are beginning, but how are you ending?

P.S. At the moment I am thinking, "It will work this way," or again, "It is time to say thank you." In between the unlivable beginning and the thought that "it works this way," a novel has unfolded, and its apparently splintered form is in fact held together from beginning to end by a progression of knowledge. This is the reason why from the moment something begins, life organizes itself in a novelistic manner. The needed encounters occur; positive accidental incidents happen. And something is making itself by itself; we are proceeding in a positive void. There are many matters, many incidents, many possible deaths, and at the end, the desire to say thank you. Of course, the story said to be of love will occupy a directional place once you have put the negative where it is, as a judging radicality. There is nothing else needing to be understood—it is a form. Nihilism stems from not-thinking nothingness. The unlivable is the fact of not being in the face of nothingness. This is a question that has seldom been dealt with by the novel. It is rare that someone says to himself or herself, "It is my fault that things are going badly for me." The idea of fault here takes on a completely different meaning from the one linking it to guilt. In fact, there is reluctance to go toward the innocence that constitutes us, and of course, poetry is the most innocent activity of all. Innocence is a form. As Hitchcock is asking, what does it mean to be innocent in a guilty world? What is the meaning of feelings spared, whole? Innocence is a form bringing along the most precise of adventures, including that which we call love in its most physical and animal form.

C.d.P. You are the only one writing about this, and even more, bringing it into literature. None wrote so well about love during that same period, love at once body and soul, animal and mental. It is one of the keys to your work.

P.S. "Key" implies "door." For instance in *Femmes*,[4] some readers have sought keys on the side of the men rather than on the side of the women. No one who has spoken to me has mentioned the very important character of the woman musician. And when it comes to *Passion fixe,* there has been even less mention of a male character who is not too far from Guy Debord with his vision of society and history involving a certain number of principles: "The falsification of the world is the becoming of the world of falsification." This is a perfectly recognizable sentence. I can copy entire passages from Lautréamont, in particular from *Poésies,* without anyone noticing. I have been doing this for a long time. I think I must have copied almost all of Ducasse[5] without anyone noticing it. I find an aesthetic satisfaction in being interviewed for television or radio when the interviewer states, "You are exaggerating when you talk about the hideous past of a crybaby humankind." But this is pure Ducasse! It is even comical to be reproached for a statement by Lautréamont, even today in a studio. There is an effervescent archive, always in the process of fusion, but it is negated when people act as if it didn't exist. Multiple identities consist in perceiving the near, the proximal, including love in which all the senses come into play. The most splintered form is alive at each moment, it has no need to gather into something finite, but it just must have truly begun. There is such a bottleneck of living people who are more dead than the dead. And it is generally proposed to end even before having begun.

And yet, isn't it strange that nowadays so much freedom is offered to the individual who truly wants to *begin*? But we observe that he or she doesn't feel like it, even though this freedom is possible without using extraordinary means but simply with a passport and the required encounters. The encounter is a form. It only requires making oneself able to do it. Multiplicity, faceted identity, multiple unity—this amounts to inventing a dramaturgy, a novel. Something is going to happen. Form is the beginning. If you are saying that form is perception, then how do you explain all those people who are not seeing, not hearing, not tasting, not touching? So now there is an inflated notion of culture within nonculture itself. What are the organs of perception that don't perceive anything? This is something that concerns me: I verify perceptions. From that moment on, we can say that we are beginning to make something.

C.d.P. You wrote in *Visions à New York,*[6] "The more I am writing the more I see," and about Picasso, "The issue is more verbal than is thought." Then you add: "We have to remember that Picasso was reading *A Season in Hell* while painting his *Demoiselles d'Avignon*." Elsewhere, you speak of Claudel and of the amazing "organ of perception" that was his language, his writing. Perception is introduced into language according to a strange economy of exchange and transformation, namely, by becoming word. As I said, we can say *table, glass of water,* but we can also say *fear, ambition,* without having experienced them. They take on a virtual existence. Thence, we can memorize them, feel them, and even really experience them, intensely experience them by combining them. The danger of language lies in it being a code. It allows us to be parsimonious in testing the real. But what you are saying is that, on the contrary, language can make visible, can reveal the visible. That it is an engine of research enabling us to feel and hear and see. Language opens, gives access to the treasure of personal experience. It enables memory to exist. You are going so far as to call it "an organ of perception." This seems to me to be advancement in the question I am posing to both myself and you. There is feedback between language and perception. But what language? It is that of the poet, of the artist, of the one who is generous with sensations.

P.S. Cézanne wrote that "since sensations are the basis of my business, I believe I am impenetrable." Sensation renders impenetrable, increasingly impenetrable.

C.d.P. Doesn't this mean "It's useless to expect an explanation from me. My business doesn't go through language"?

P.S. Of course. It means "I owe you the truth in painting, and I will tell it to you." As for me, I am saying, "I owe you the truth in novels, and I will tell it to you." What matters is the truth of sensations and redirecting commands.

C.d.P. When I built the water tower into a tower of Babel, I could see it as the redirecting of a functional plan. At that time, the wish to get free of the yoke, of the visual spread of the accumulated technical necessity, led me to redirecting. I was asking myself the question of the tyranny of the language of technical function that prevented me to see. Could architecture escape from this, escape from feeling that it has to dwell solely in the realm of the useful? The modern orthodox form has always been a response to a constraint. As for me, I never first see the form of an object. I see the form of hollowness. I see that an object contains and makes possible an empty form in which we are living.

One day I found out that Lao Tzu had written the same thing: "My house is not the wall, it is not the ground, it is not the roof; it is the emptiness between these things because that is where I am dwelling." I came across this text and was moved during the eighties. It was what I had been trying to say since 1972 without being understood. I was always told: but that is negative, your thing about emptiness, space. From that day forth I have been citing Lao Tzu, and since then, everyone understands me. I am told that this is perfectly fine. Emptiness, thanks to Lao Tzu, is no longer perceived as negative. It has become the formula.

Recently I was reading the text of a 1939 lecture by Frank Lloyd Wright delivered in London to some students. He suddenly told them that he was about to make a revelation. This was that he had once read a sentence by Lao Tzu that influenced him. It was this same sentence about emptiness. This got my interest, and all the more so that Wright added in his lecture: "When I read this sentence, I held the book to my heart and told myself: that's my secret; I must not reveal it to anyone. The whole of my life, in my architecture, I have felt the void." And a bit of a ham, he adds: "Today, I am giving you my secret."

For me, that is clearly how I felt at the beginning of the seventies, when I had distanced myself from architectural culture and was on a journey far away from all references. From 1967 to 1970, I contemplated giving up architecture. I saw it as authoritarian; I saw it as a manner of occupying space in an authoritarian, frozen manner, one that didn't leave any choice to people. Well, that is what I was telling myself. To build seemed to me a trite idea. To turn away from it, yes. I thought only the logic of objects was going to reign everywhere, that there was no longer any need for architecture.

P.S. Did you think at that moment, even if only for an instant, that by denying the need for architecture, you were denying in the same breath the need for nature?

C.d.P. I wasn't conscious of it. But it is true, and what followed proved it. Except that at that time in my life, the modern world seemed to me to be, on the contrary, like a second nature, artificial and fascinating, on which the traditional discipline of architecture had no effect. I thought that technical logic was bound to dominate absolutely.

So in 1970, when I took up the idea of architecture again, it was on the basis of the notion of space: I am interested in the city as form. I saw the water tower as a poetical landmark in the landscape of a new city that I knew was to be formless. I wrote at that time: "The techno-economics logic has invaded the world; the identity of all countries will be one with the numbers of its economy." In 1967 I was telling myself that I should no longer do architecture, but in 1970 I saw it as an absolute necessity in the face of the sole economic and analytical logic, in the face of numbers. It was needed in order to live differently from the life this technical calculator was constructing. At that same moment, there was a scientific current among architects, a current claiming that nothing matters outside of systems, neither form nor space. When I reflected about architecture, I found myself outside the field of language; I felt like a schizophrenic, divided in two. On the one hand there was writing, on the other the projects. It had to be one or the other. Two different areas of the brain. It took me a long time to be able to talk about a project in a simple, nontheoretical manner, to put the language, sensations, technique, and spatial form together. For instance, after the construction of the water tower, I was asked to write an explanatory text, but I couldn't do it. The text was leading me into a world of reflection on the framework and the vegetal, on form and filtrated transparency, motion and landmark, geometry and nature. There was no end to it; commentary couldn't exhaust the visible. I stopped. That was a beneficial experience for an architect! Another side of the brain had been at work. There had been a dream and a vision of the city, and an idea of form. I had renounced the idea that form was against life.

P.S. And since the soul is the form of the body, you were reformulating the issue of the body in the face of architecture.

5. "Manufacturability"

P.S. The latest concerns have to do with the "prefabricability" of human beings.

C.d.P. In fifty years, that which was nature has become increasingly artificial. Nature is now the object of calculation and of a relation of power. The industrial revolution has turned a world that was basically carved out of nature into a produced world. The world, matter, had been shaped and arranged in a unique manner in every place. Now, the greater part of the matter surrounding us is made up of technical objects, molded or extruded substances—the products of industrial machines. It is an entirely different way of looking at the world. You buy, you use, you throw away. There's no reuse.

The programmed mastery of the planet, of nature, that is the accomplishment of the Western idea of modernity. In 1949, in "The Question concerning Technology," when Heidegger talks of that which "sets-upon" nature, he is not thinking of genetics.[1] He is thinking, for instance, of the dam, of the electrical plant—a forced modeling of nature. At present, technology is aimed at the artificial production of nature. When it comes to travel, distance communication, shelter, eating, prolonging life, we are already animals with prostheses, surrounded by machines.

To build a building, to lay out a place, now involves arranging objects, plugging in or assembling networks or components on one ground or another. There are fluxes and connections in between today's networks and objects. The notion of space, the principle that used to assemble everything, was issued from the previously arranged, carved, dug-up world. Now, under the reign of technology, the notion of space seems at times archaic. And yet, archaic doesn't mean out-of-date. Our bodies are very archaic but also very actual forms. They are originary forms. What happened to this notion of space, and how did it happen? For instance, what were Le Corbusier's thoughts on the city? He applied technical reasoning, the industrial method, to the city. He asked how does it function, how can mass production be achieved, how does it circulate: water, electricity, trucks, pedestrians, houses, dwellings. In order to think rationally about buildings, they have to be large, repetitive, autonomous, and produced like technical objects. He separates them. Then he thinks about health, greenery, factory, leisure. He wants to make neighborhoods that are also separated. Then he has to speak of the street. He knows that the essence of the city is the street. While still very young, he wrote a book about it before World War I, a book that wasn't published and in which he defended the street and place against the viewpoint of the German engineers and hygienists who, after a fire, had disfigured his hometown, La Chaux-de-Fonds. They rebuilt it with separated buildings that no longer defined the streets. Le Corbusier was traumatized by the destruction of a past that he had not known, that of his mother's village. He praised streets and place. Then strangely, after the war, after a stay in Munich and a few years of reflection, he gradually became a proponent of opening the landscape of the street and airing it, of putting green spaces in between tall buildings. At the outset he saw it as a health concern. He claimed that streets were dirty, dark, and too narrow. He felt that all the existing Paris streets should be wiped out. He saw this as a moral, radical, total act. Things must be unified. What he hated about the street was that it was impure and couldn't be controlled, that it was made up of individualities. It collected everything, the past and the future, the collective and the private, into a single form. A form always at once the same and different—it was unpredictable, it carried timelessness in itself, it underwent transformations, and it was at once place and motion. So Le Corbusier wanted to eliminate it and replace it with a series of tubes and freeways. The import of this gesture has never been pointed out. Likewise ignored is the ancient gesture of the invention of the street somewhere in the Middle East, perhaps at Milet by Hipodamos. At any rate, the doctrine of elimination of the street that seems to have been the product of a marginal utopianism in the 1930s was to have an international success after World War II. This is quite surprising when we think about it. The whole world adopts the program; streets are eliminated. They are leveled off in Singapore, in Peking. They are no longer respected in Manhattan, in Paris. Everywhere, building or rebuilding is done without them, whether it be after the bombs or the bulldozers, with an optimistic hatred of everything that was there before. This was a trusting hope. In the face of this, we must also remember that in the rare locales where modern urbanism wasn't applied, monumentalism was practiced in its stead. I am thinking of the huge boulevards of Ceaucescu's Bucharest. The street cannot be a doctrine. It calls for an answer.

P.S. I am struck by the increasingly evident separation between the street for automobile circulation and the street artificially reserved for pedestrians. Most of the streets I knew thirty years ago had only small points of visibility in relation to one's position. These streets, which used to call for adventure with their many dark corners, are now very well lighted and reserved solely for pedestrians. The more such streets become showcases in themselves, the less happens in them, though pedestrians walking late at night were also scarce in the streets of the past. This brings to mind Baudelaire's magnificent verse:

> The lovely hour that is the felon's friend.[2]

Increasingly, the street will become either a conduit for cars or a place of commerce, of shops. After a certain hour at night, all the lights are still on but there is no longer anybody around. It is interesting to walk in this no-man's-land where it seems that nothing can happen. We are circulating and nothing happens. This proclivity to avoid, as much as possible, the happening of any event in the center of cities resurfaces the form of violence in those places that lag behind technologically in the staging of the human spectacle. We should not be surprised if the centralizing pressure of the street, whether it be motorized or illuminated and pedestrian (which means the elimination of the pedestrian since he or she gets stuck when alone) engenders a growing peripheral violence on account of the artificial calm installed at its center.

C.d.P. Walter Benjamin was meandering in Paris at the same time as avant-garde meetings were being held on the topic of how to rebuild entirely mastered cities. Benjamin first looked at the city as enchantment, as the Surrealists did, and then he saw in it the "concretization" enabling us to understand the history of the nineteenth century. He wanted to write a book about it, but he wasn't able to finish because the project was too big. The enormous amount of his preparatory work has survived. And while Benjamin wandered in the streets and the boulevards and worked at the library, another man was interested in the center of the nineteenth-century capital. This was Le Corbusier. He wished to make the center disappear. During these same years, Le Corbusier drew up the Voisin plan for Paris in which he proposed to wipe out the whole city center. He explained the need to go even further than Haussmann and to see big and far. Walter Benjamin didn't like Haussmann, he kept on berating him, and yet Benjamin did also talk about the future, about revolution; he spoke in the name of the people. He was interested in passageways, in the boulevards manifesting the concrete history of techniques, commerce, urban life. He was Beaudelairean and at the same time he wanted to be materialist, Marxist. He was filled with contradictions. For him the city as physical reality was nonidealized, material history. What Le Corbusier was preparing was not at all imaginary; it can be found in his proposals and plans. This is the open cities concept of state capitalism and socialism. But then the states ended up handing them over to the private sector, which was to seize this limitless open territory. The unpredictable was to take back its rights, but in confusion, in the fuzzy addition of carried-over rules and decisions and all the while through the heightened efficiency of broad-based business. This began what I have called Age III of the city of which I spoke earlier. It is a maelstrom that we no longer know how to deal with and transform. Are we still able to act, or is it that the will can no longer make an impact?

The other day, someone who was present during our conversation told me: "This is interesting; you seem to want to change the city. That is surprising. For us, for the younger generations, the city is not an object of reflection or of change." Indeed, it is now possible to see the city as a new nature, an artificial one, an environment to which we have to adapt, but without the means or the reasons to transform it or to think of a future for it. It is argued that there are many things that matter more. And yet, this argument is only makeshift logic. After all, this environment does exist and the countless business mechanisms that move it seem to be beyond anyone's control. This future is thus not thought to be a worthwhile subject to dwell on. So, this member of the audience was surprised to hear us thinking in terms of the future.

In contrast, an architect who was asking me questions told me, "The extent that you are interested in the history of the city is pretty strange." And he even tried to link this to the fact that I always keep all my early drawings for my projects, and he wondered if this was not a case of conservatism! For me, the drawing is an integral part of the thinking process, and the beginning is as useful and important as the end. The project exists both in the head and in reality; it is a progression and a whole. For them, it only lies in the final image. Doesn't thinking of history as cumbersome and finding an interest in it surprising amount to a wish to suppress time, to suppress the vision of time, the idea, even imprecise, of a perspective on the future? And doesn't holding that to be aware of the itinerary to creation is a sort of conservatism amount to a denial of time, of antecedents? Doesn't it amount to a frozen present, a laborious present, the one I am experiencing even in my own work in the form of the mercantile aspect of commissions?

During the last century, the future took over, and the idea of transforming the city, the world, became a major obsession. Today, the idea couldn't be further from people's minds. In our economy-dominated time, it is rare to find people ready to create projects for a future of more than four years. Four years seems to be the limit. It is the profit on the investment that seems to form the only visible horizon, the only control. The rest is unpredictable and thus uninteresting.

P.S. Marx thought that once the world was interpreted it had to be transformed. This world has been transformed, increasingly so to the point that Debord was right in asserting that the present-day slave feels compelled to be absolutely modern.[3] This is a turnaround in perspective as a future realized at each moment proves that capitalism has been extremely underestimated by utopians, revolutionaries, humanists, by all those who were the "righteous" of metaphysics and who find themselves without any defenses when the light of day shines on the horizon of appropriation and the general social setup. We can no longer expect anything else from the vision of a world to be transformed but a redoubling of servitude. This is the very thing that has occurred blatantly these last twenty years and will of course worsen. We are only at the beginning.

The absence of future corresponds to an expelling of the past and the forcing of a constant present to renew itself. This is because the creation of needs is unavoidably accompanied by the creation of new needs. No matter what you just purchased, you will need to buy something else right away so as to be more modern, more with it. Grafted need implies its doubling.

This reminds me of a conversation I had twenty years ago with Sir Jimmy Goldsmith, who was at the time the owner of the weekly *L'Express*. He was mistaken about my identity. He tried to engage me in a discussion (before looking at my file and noticing that it wouldn't work) by asking me if I thought we needed to apply Leninist methods to the expansion of liberalism. I replied that this seemed to me an excellent idea, and he didn't understand that I was being ironic and was anticipating his next question. After this, he asked who did I think was the most important thinker of the twentieth century, and I answered with a straight face, Pavlov.

Thus Goldsmith unknowingly was a rational Marxist. There are ads today that show Marx smoking a cigar, Mao with a bowler hat heading a bank. This imagery, the hold images have on us, must be having an overwhelming influence on architecture that, in principle, functions first on a possibility of the sacred. But we are in an era that is no longer modern but planetary, where *the horizon no longer generates rays from itself* (Heidegger). To me it seems that the real issue is that architecture is deprived of the sacred.

We shouldn't be surprised if the body is declared indefinitely replaceable and that the small remaining human part is declared superfluous. Bodies would be indefinitely replaceable because they are now apt to be manufactured. Inasmuch as the body has been assigned to the realm of the quantifiable, it is required to correspond to an image. We are in a detour of history where the question of birth and death takes on an entirely different dimension. It is a mutation in the way a possible construction of a space could remind the few human beings present of its ephemerality. Now the aim is the eradication of this small surviving interpellation that reminds us that life is short, death is unavoidable, and time is precious. This new world is formless due to a peculiar fluidity and viscosity preventing fixed landmarks. As Pascal noted, when all are hurrying toward excess, the one who stops also points at it. Or again as Karl Krauss put it, "If someone has something to say, let him stand up and be silent." Stopping can be a major event. If you stop, you are immediately asked if you are reactionary or conservative since "Mister Stock Market" and his family are eager to remind you that the new must be constantly produced, that we cannot stop for a single instant. In the global era we are in the process of entering, it is frustrating that all discourses are still referenced on the modern. It is very rare to hear a discourse that is participating in the establishment of a new era without using the language that came from before it.

C.d.P. The core figure, the model, is the revolution along with the recycling of its image. A rupture must be replayed; we are required to state that everything is in the process of changing. This rupture must be periodically replayed along different cycles for different professions, for instance, every ten years or every year. People speak of generations. Without this Oedipus played on the revolutionary mode, we have the impression of lacking an identity. This theater established itself when the idea of revolution became disqualified, when there was no longer any possible ideological opposition to capitalism.

And yet, there remains an unequal world that has hardened as it moved into the territory and the city. Of course, the material world and bodies still exist, and it is in that realm that today the control over space is played out. On the one hand, some zones have been made secure while, on the other, whole segments of cities have been abandoned. The class struggle is inscribed into space to the point that there is now a trend to privatize chunks of cities, to put up walls, to close up. We need key cards to enter into some parts of towns. We see this already in Los Angeles and São Paulo, and this will soon happen in Paris, in Europe, if we do not take action.

P.S. All ideological formulas are now out-of-date in relation to what is happening. If I decree the end of history or the end of ideologies, any response I might get would be of no import. The protest might be moving, but its only effect would be to actually reinforce the system, particularly in its predatory aspects. It is a system that disdainfully shames anyone who dares express his or her horror of this process. Protest is ineffective. So what could be effective given that I don't think we are living through an apocalypse or the end of history and ideologies? Debord argues that everyone is plotting in favor of the established order. Revolutionary theory is the enemy of revolutionary ideology, and ideology knows it. This is one of the theses of the *Society of the Spectacle*[4] that hasn't been paid enough attention to.

I come back to Heidegger. The surveillance of space cannot be conceived without some sort of surveillance of time. It follows that space has to be organized in a particular way, a task to which are invited specialists, technicians—I no longer dare say artists, but it is possible that there are still some around. These will increasingly be asked to have this nonknowledge of time and to bend to the programs for the managing of space.

In order to know where we stand, we have to remember that we are in the process of moving from the *place* to the *site*. Not long ago, the street was a place of happenstance. The project aimed at eliminating, as much as possible, useless gestures, unexplainable encounters, gratuitousness in all its forms, has to absolutely keep track of the movements of the individual locked in the program's representation of time. It would be good to reread the great surrealist texts that are all devoted to the street. When André Breton decided that something was going to happen to him, he went into the street and encountered Nadja. He inserted photographs in his narrative to emphasize the street's state of receptivity where facades, graffiti, all that which is said unwitting, speak to the walker who thus finds in the asphalt the point through which things flee or appear. It is the same in *Le paysan de Paris*,[5] in which Aragon was still in a state of existential interpellation. Later on, there was the repression of the invention of a subject able to pass from one scene to another, from one neighborhood to another, from one lover to another, from one state of mind to another. All the art of that time, all the art of a Picasso was built on this, on the exercise of freedom. The art of drifting.

C.d.P. Where we find ourselves . . .

P.S. . . . in Paris. Paris is thus a city whose history is as much of the nineteenth century as of the middle of the twentieth, with subjects, individuals, who invented a manner of being that was the same and yet different in different places in the course of a day. So why shouldn't we have this relative discipline instead of the nine-to-five drudgery that has again become the norm? It is this expectant temporal relationship that brings on one's spatial availability.

C.d.P. I think that the conflict at the root of Debord's rejection of Constant . . .[6]

P.S. . . . lies here.

C.d.P. Constant was still an artist who then created his great structures floating over the planet.

P.S. Even though that isn't the goal.

C.d.P. These structures imagine another world. Constant is still a structural utopian while, at that moment, Guy Debord was rejecting the urbanism said to be unitary.

P.S. This is because situationist urbanism denied the subject.

C.d.P. It is in order to start again with the subject that Debord calls upon the experience of drifting. Everything is played out here: in the idea of chance, of unpredictability.

P.S. This means that we do not know ahead of time. If you do not know, you are putting yourself into a state of receptivity in which something will happen to you. I can vouch for this because my own individual practice testifies that this kind of technique works in all sorts of situations. But everything has been made so as to thwart this. And yet, what would happen if we imagined an architecture based on the notion that something could happen?

The mutation through which we are living is, in my opinion, increasingly sociological, sociocompulsive, sociomaniacal.[7] The socio-addicted covers with asphalt any question pertaining to existence. A person showing lack of adhesion to the sociocompulsive vision of the world is thus seen as heretic.

C.d.P. With what are they replacing existential questioning?

P.S. With the fact that they require us to speak in terms of the social desires and needs that they impose on us. If you do not feel these, you begin to appear as an enemy of society, society being defined as a god or as an absolute subjectivity. The global era is the realization of anthropomorphism, of absolute subjectivity, that is, of the absence of sense, and then soon the advent of senselessness. Nietzsche expressed this so well with his "God is dead." The devaluation of suprasensible values and then the devaluation of the sensible lead us into absurdity and senselessness.

Are we going to be able to think this senselessness through injections of sense? Evidently not, since these injections would immediately be dissolved in the absence of sensibility and sense that leads to senselessness. Thus today, even before speaking, we need to be able to ascertain the sensitivity of those with whom we are talking because there's a possibility that they aren't feeling anything. Often, it happens to me that I am talking here or there, but I always make sure that I am talking to the speaker, to the recorder, to the camera, no matter what the situation.

C.d.P. You mean that those who are listening or those who will listen are not there.

P.S. That's the point, and it is glaring that, according to whether there is or isn't a camera, the talk and the nonlistening itself change. The subject today must be very able to understand that he or she is speaking without a recording in a total void. That is a new situation. And it is the reason why, since we are entering a global era, I am so interested in that which preceded modern times.

I wrote a book on Dante's *Divine Comedy*[8] that has been forgotten by modern times as well as demonized and, in my opinion, has much to tell us precisely because it is in the situation of the geologically repressed. It is Dante who writes about the "visible word." Hell is a funnel for clichés, for repetition of the objects; hell is the punishment of the damned. The damned are going toward aphasia, a more and more frozen mumbling. In contrast, purgatory, very analytically from this viewpoint, is a long road made up of ledges. Souls pass from circles rooted in aphasia to platforms that are stations, the aim being to reach a nature that has never fallen since it is terrestrial paradise. But within this travel between the ledges, the "visible word" brings back art. There are sculptures, frescoes, flying sentences. These poor dead souls have to reeducate themselves, expiate their pain, their sins. These sins are always the same: envy, jealousy, pride, laziness. Envy is the main one; it is essential.

The "visible word" implies a rediscovery of speech, of the song, of the street, of architecture.

So, to come back to the formless world you were speaking about, it is the locus of a programmed erotic delay. It is obvious that the manufactured being, a being quantifiable in function of what is expected of him or her, implies as much as possible the suppression of pleasure. Yes, pleasure can be bought, but one must absolutely not reach a state of fulfillment because the negativity that it would involve could threaten the cave where all this apparatus tends to install itself. Baudelaire's *Artificial Paradises*[9] comes to mind here. He expressed some essential things and explained that the poet's mother is terrified by his birth. That is why he was censured until 1949 for the first two poems of *Flowers of Evil,* "To the Reader" and "Consecration":

> When by an edict of the sovereign powers
> The Poet enters this indifferent world,

His mother, spurred to blasphemy by shame,
Clenches her fists at a condoling God:
"Why not have given me a brood of snakes."[10]

C.d.P. You wrote about the "visible word": "what each person is prompted to represent to himself or herself under the sway of verbal sexual stimulation is absolutely private. It is never the same for two persons." This is a sentence from an interview you gave about eroticism. I transcribe this by generalizing the erotic pulse to our lives, since this makes me think of films. All the cinematographic renderings of a novel evidence what you are saying here about sexuality. When reading a narrative, a story, we always visualize it, even in spite of ourselves. We spatialize situations. And we always notice when viewing a film based on a novel that we had a completely different picture of the places and the atmosphere. This "absolutely private" is never the same for two individuals. It comes out of our experience of desire, of space. We imagine a context effortlessly, and we only become aware of it when confronted by someone else's vision. Writing has the extraordinary power to bring up in us a continent of memory, of experience, of sensations. It is absolutely superior to film. As soon as there is a situation, we can't help but visualize, spatialize, the narrative. Fiction is natural to us. This fact is at once banal and extraordinary. When we work in architecture it is on this continent that we are led to dwell, this space and this visible that were brought up by language, by desire, by the order for the project.

Thus, we could say that we have language on one side and the visible and space on the other. I see them as two environments in which we are moving, like air and water. They are not hybrid, and yet we are like fish and bird at once or in turn, one after the other. There is a surface contact between these two milieus, there is constant exchange, but we are in either one or the other. I became aware of this quite a long time ago during the seventies while reading Julia Kristeva and her theory of intertextuality according to which a text always responds to another text. I would add that a space responds to a space.

The notion that we never work, create, from nothing but always from a constituted field applies as much to space as to text. The visible and space form a specific field, a store that makes the architectural dream possible. In between space and language there is total foreignness and a permanent communication. The contact surface is necessary because of the need to transmit and to speak. Language is a memory learned and shared, and we transform it into a unique personal treasure. Each person's idea of space and of the visible are private memories, emotional experiences, that the built world, the cities, help to transform into shared memory. It was thus not stupid to say that architecture works like a language, that it aims to be a language. But when this was said at the end of the sixties, mechanical reductionism quickly raised its head. The formulations of semiotics did not grasp the specific mode of existence of space and of the visible such as perceptions, sensations, light, geometry, movements, etc. For instance, that which partakes of shared memory in the visible and in space, and that which does not, is very subtle and difficult to understand. And this is precisely the traces we are following in a project.

For centuries, the central idea of architecture consisted in sharing a memory that could be grasped by all, thanks to its nature as public art. There were defined codes that enabled a society, an era, to recognize itself. That is why the Renaissance went in search of antiquity with the aim of again dipping into this shared, phantasmagoric memory.

It is amazing that the reference, the model, for a long time was located in the origins, in antiquity, and that during the last century, the reference became the end, the image of the future. The passion for the *future* was born in the twentieth century. From that time on, shared memory ceased to be the obligatory reference for creating. It even had to be ignored. Now, things are different. We dwell in the present, without any shared reference. We see caricatural pastiches of the past or, on the contrary, the erasure of all roots, of all antecedents. History is either turned into conserves or else transformed into an amusement park. But in the city, history is also the future.

History structures all thought; it always comes back, even if today so many people don't know where they, and what they are doing, came from.

C.d.P. Architecture is time made concrete, or as Bachelard held, that is what space does. When we are building, and we see things come out of the earth, it is impossible to remain pessimistic; we have to act. As Hölderlin would say, when danger is growing, so also is the possibility of rescue.

P.S. The more sociomania is expanding, the more the freedom of the individual could be saved. We are at the dawn of unheard-of freedom for the individual. But does she or he want this freedom? That is a new question.

6. Adventure of Language, Time, Body

P.S. In preparation for today's discussion I wrote down "Café," "Nocturnal," "Apollinaire," "Emotion," and also "Planet."

C.d.P. Planet, screen, image—thousands of images. I am thinking of a text you wrote titled "The Erotic Delay," which ends with the following sentence: "Any image, even the most violent one, is still always a pious image." We can't argue with an image. We can't reason with it. In architecture, more now than ever, we travel with evoking, betraying images that are supposed to represent real places, new and unknown buildings, and give the effect of reality that is out of sync and fake. This is unavoidable. Our world has grown; we cannot go and see what has been done everywhere. Things, places are known through images; they are the ones circulating. More and more we are producing illusional virtual images close to reality but showing buildings that don't exist or don't exist yet. In fact, it is only when we are in the place itself that we can experience the truth of the space. But the image nowadays is worth more than the real. It points it out; it chooses it; it claims to be reality's spirit. In contrast to a text, we can't reason with an image: it either catches our attention or not. There are even architectural projects whose images have been shown in all the books, but when one accidentally comes upon them in place, they are on waste ground; they don't have any use; they were made solely to be photographed. The effect of the image is one of fixation, seduction. This is what advertising is based on. The image induces a stop. It might be accompanied by a commentary, but language is not the dominant element here. Film, TV, and the photograph have transformed our relationship with the visible world. Film consecrates the hegemony of the producer of the image over the script writer who is treated as a tradesperson. I am thinking of a certain filmmaker who, during a press conference, aggressively responded to a journalist's question with "You still belong to an ancient world where people were still reading." In a nineteenth-century household, all knowledge, all news, entertainment, stories, everything that today has become spectacle, had to essentially pass through the written word, through books, almanacs. Now the news is on television in the form of images. And the image always fascinates us like the unveiling of a prohibition to gaze.

P.S. Just a comment here. I use the formula that might appear extremely paradoxical on the subject of pornography . . .

C.d.P. Yes, the "erotic delay."

P.S. Pornography is today's religion. We've gone from Saint Sulpice to pornography.

C.d.P. The image, now that was a great debate. Can God be represented? And during the Renaissance, there were representations of the body and then dissection, that is, the right to show the nude and then to open up cadavers. There was fascination. It was an important moment in history that gave a quasi-scientific authority to painting. Painting had an effect of truth. We went from medieval representation to the Renaissance when the representation of the body became "realistic"; I don't think that there were many nudes before that. There were nudes in hell and in paradise in Hieronymus Bosch. These were the damned but also the glorious nudes. But now, the images produced by new software raise troubling questions. Is it built or not? But you were talking about representation.

P.S. About the industrialization of pornography.

C.d.P. As I cited in our last conversation, you wrote: "What each person is prompted to represent to himself or herself under the sway of verbal sexual stimulation is absolutely private. It is never the same for two persons."

P.S. For two private parties to meet each other today, they'll need some luck! It happens very rarely and always verbally.

C.d.P. Thus, the representation of the world is given to us in two modes. On the one hand, today's images are landmarks of authority. One cannot be for or against; one cannot speak of them. Language stumbles; the matter is judged through vision. Images are always beyond or beneath words. Images are the materials of advertising, of business, of propaganda. On the other hand, there is the language of commentary. But it often only serves to attract the gaze, to point to the image. We are in two places at once as well as in perpetual motion between the world of images, of the screen, and of the one we perceive as reality. We experience the anesthetizing euphoria of the distanceless. There, the physical and the material are no longer a problem because they have been turned into spectacle. And yet, in spite of this, the body has not disappeared.

P.S. No, but it is one of humankind's old dreams to make it disappear.

C.d.P. But then Saint John could no longer write, "The word made flesh."

P.S. Everyone doesn't agree with this. It's an enormous claim.

C.d.P. The whole of the movement of rational thought in the West has tended to detach the flesh from the spirit. There was the necessity of producing a language that could be the stuff of thinking no longer submitted to the body, to sensations, to perceptions. There was the necessity of producing an agreement that would no longer involve the body, this rigorously private, idiosyncratic matter, never identical for two persons. That was the precondition through which experimental observation and science were attained.

P.S. Someone who maintains the private before all else becomes extremely suspect.

C.d.P. There is art and there is love, and these encompass the whole of subjectivity. Here, the private is absolute. It's a principle that is destructive for the social tie, that is not assimilable.

P.S. They are not expected by the sociocracy.

C.d.P. Would you not agree that we are describing a status of art that slowly and gradually emerged after the [French] Revolution at the time of the Romantics, and even more so afterward? Artists no longer had to kowtow to anyone or to claim the goodness of the king. They were only asked to be alone, unique, themselves.

P.S. That was to cost them dearly.

C.d.P. The artist was to gradually embody the subjective and absolute existential adventure. In contrast, the architect was on the constructive side, a positive one for society. This created a distance between architectural culture and literature, music and painting. Architecture remained dominated by the academies and politics for a long time. Its history is heavy with transmission, initiation, and corporations ever since the Masonic lodges of the cathedrals. Its responsibility is building for someone else. Artists have no need to construct the world.

For the last two centuries, they have challenged this supposed construction. They have claimed the preeminence of private adventure against all, and in particular they offer this absolute experience to everyone. Of course, since the nineteenth century there have been many movements attempting to bring closer, to reconcile, to unite, art and architecture, art and society, art and industry, etc. Generally, they tried to do this by using an idea of social utility. The Bauhaus School and Russian Constructivism brought about a genuine meeting among architecture, art, and technique. Today, there is a set of technological and economic mechanisms that are building a world in which architecture is marginalized. Architecture thenceforth illustrates your "theory of exceptions."[1] Each commission and each site are unique. There is no longer any shared doctrine, style, or rules; there is no longer any functional universal solution. In this changing and unpredictable world, the "case by case" puts architects in the same situations as authors, even when they are anonymous or mediocre. When does the notion of author begin? Not too long ago you answered my question with "Dante."

P.S. He was the first to identify himself within the body of the very thing he was making.

C.d.P. It's not with the Renaissance . . .

P.S. It's not the same thing. The Renaissance was already part of modern times. Dante was not a modern. It is an issue of periodization.

C.d.P. That is . . .

P.S. We are exiting the modern period. We are no longer in it. We are entering the global era. The problem is to know how. Are we entering it walking backward or with lucidity? Most human beings, for reasons that can be explained, arrive in the third millennium with a nineteenth-century imaginary. This can be proven. How strange . . . Let us come back for a moment to the beginning of the twentieth century, around 1905, 1906, 1907. There is already someone manifesting himself brilliantly: Apollinaire. This poet has obviously been nourished by his predecessors, including Baudelaire, Rimbaud, Mallarmé, but he has also been fed by an ancient library, and suddenly he starts to say things about a painter who wasn't expected and who was called Picasso. Apollinaire's writings on Picasso must be reread. They had a great, fervent friendship interrupted by Apollinaire's death at age thirty-eight—very young—in 1918. And Picasso, as he was slowly dying after his glorious life that had been linked to architecture (since it is in function of an invisible architecture that everything in his work happened), asks (among his last words): "But where is Apollinaire?"—at the end of his life, Picasso was thinking that everything already existed in an absolutely intense moment from the very beginning. Today, we are talking about globalization, but as for me, I think that we are entering an unworld. In truth, it might appear that human beings are no longer living on the same planet.

Picasso demonstrates that in the midst of intense misunderstandings, he can paint a portrait of Apollinaire or of Kahnweiler that no longer has anything to do with portraiture as it had been thought up to then, and at the same time, he can paint, and paint very well, completely classical traditional portraits. Thus he is someone in the process of dividing in two. Picasso is indubitably the greatest artist of the twentieth century. We either accept this and realize the depth of the impact of his experience, or alternatively, we decide that nothing happened. I am using him as an example because it seems to me he triumphed over all nineteenth-century types of ideologies ("doomed genius," etc.).

C.d.P. We are talking about authors, and it is Picasso who comes up. He is the one who carried his time the furthest, but he also sought to work in earnest with history and the past and to look at these in a different manner.

P.S. Apollinaire himself tells us, in an astonishing manner, that for Picasso, "The world is as he represents it."[2] It follows an entirely different perception of time, space, the human body, the body's image, and the manner in which it manifests its presence. A cubist portrait of Picasso has a real intensity; it is a resemblance that doesn't resemble. And yet, if you compare his very classical portrait of Apollinaire with his bandage and cap with his cubist portrait of Apollinaire, you can well wonder in what way this is the same man and why does Picasso insist on claiming he is the same? The reality of the classical portrait is inferior to the other one, which is already a counterattack forewarning that the image is to lose its power of resembling and to become something else. This doesn't mean that resemblance ceases. This particular event happened at the moment when the photograph, the film, the image in the broad sense of the term, was to enter into full expansion and arrive to encryption. We lived this long history of the image during the nineteenth century so as to end up in digitalization. Computerization—but basically on what backdrop? That of numbers, thus on a backdrop of absence rather than presence.

I am quite struck by the fact that no one is really looking at Picasso's work. It is as if his work never existed. With Picasso's collages of bits of papers, the division of which he was the operator remains misunderstood. No one seems to want to ask in what way this body is Picasso: naked chest, provocateur, women, pseudocommunist, corridas, hats, genius artist who let himself ironically become a spectacle in a manner for which he was often criticized. They say that he "came back" to figurative painting and to classicism while at the same time he was pursuing things that have nothing to do with this sort of appearance. He did this the whole of his life, from one side to the other. I think that this has not yet been completely understood. At the beginning of the twentieth century there was a project in which poetry and painting were closely intertwined: Apollinaire and Picasso. Then the butchery of 1914–18 put a stop to it. There is no French village without a monument to its dead. The problem is to know what the Third Republic was, the one that lasted for quite a long time, up to 1940. The other day, I was at the Lyon prefecture where Sadi Carnot, the president of the French Republic, was assassinated by an Italian anarchist. They show you the parlor where he died, stretched out on a sofa. A very kitsch painting hangs on the wall showing the event of his death in 1895, in the midst of a fairly imposing architectural ensemble inaugurated in 1890. This setting is an example of past republican glory, one that bewilders us today. In this decor, we imagine gentlemen and ladies, prefects, intrigues, the whole of the literature of the time. At the same time, it is entirely deserted, unlivable. It is a vision of that which still takes itself to be a world, one hundred and ten years later.

I had the same feeling in Washington, D.C., at the Capitol. Its columns seem to be made of marble powder; it is nineteenth-century style in all its splendor, a vision of past civilization. But the museum next door, designed by Pei, slices through the landscape. Pei obviously has looked at Picasso's paintings of pasted papers, and he has a Chinese culture. He also made a mark of the same order with the pyramids of the Louvre; it is an operation, like a knife cut.

C.d.P. In Washington this Pei building is one of the first convincing examples of a construction anchored in the continuity of modern architecture but that nonetheless perfectly fits in the classical path. This is the path designed by the French urbanist Jean-Baptiste L'Enfant, into which Pei's building emerges even more pertinently than would a construction in the classical style. In contrast, modern buildings had always previously stood in opposition to classical design. There was a struggle of principles between modern architecture and the existing city. Modern architecture actually emerged in opposition to the classical city. When Le Corbusier built his building at Harvard, he set it diagonally in between two streets like an object with its own logic, indifferent to the city, even fighting it. It was as if the building was there as an avant-garde to prepare the city for the advent of an entirely different city. In truth, Le Corbusier, and his disciples who explained this to me, had the certitude that the city around it, the "already-there," was always and every-where destined to be leveled off. And the modern building al-ways had to show the new direction that had to be followed.

P.S. But you agree on the knife-edge appearance of Pei's inter-vention?

C.d.P. Yes, Pei's building cuts because it is between the great es-planade and a diagonal avenue; thus it is the site that provided Pei with his theme as the building sits on a triangular terrain. He makes use of the triangular geometry with a set of pure lines and planes that give the building its abstract simplicity and autonomy. Previously, the treatment of the angle into a fine vertical line was forbidden in architecture. Among the classi-cists there was a saying that "the infinitely small doesn't exist in architecture." This fine cut is at once the modernity of the building and the condition of its historical link, of its insertion into a classical site. Well done!

P.S. I am using him as example for this reason. In Washington you exit the Capitol, where you are crushed by power in the sense that it is derisory, it is a point of saturation with plaster and lousy frescoes, and then, suddenly, this blade, this ship's stem appears. It is as if you introduced a ship into the city, as if the ocean entered where it had no business.

C.d.P. And this creates the effect of breathing.

P.S. Yes, of breathing, of freedom. So it is all the more interest-ing that when I was there, inside Pei's building, there was an exhibition of Chinese art. Here were coincidences between this architectural knife cut in the midst of Washington, D.C., and the Chinese statues that had come from so far away. It was a fabulous breath of fresh air, which brings me back to my idea that we don't necessarily live on the same planet in the course of our lives. That building gives us the feeling that we are enter-ing the plurality of worlds.

C.d.P. The same holds for the representation of the cosmos. We used to represent the earth as flat, unique, and total. Then came the image of the solar system in which the earth circles the sun. In the twentieth century the number of systems exploded into "worlds," and now each day we are exploring new and more distant horizons. Unity is a thing of the past.

P.S. Using Pei as an example, it seems to me that architecture will from now on be able to intervene in a manner at once very new and very ancient, as I have just tried to say about the museum in Washington that suddenly makes Chinese space appear. The architect then can signal through constraints, as you have done yourself with the Cité de la Musique or with your tower in New York. You point, in spite of the constraint, toward something that is a meditation on time. Your tower has, for instance, a "Fragonard" color, it has a "French" elegance in the midst of New York. A French person in New York, a Chinese in Washington, D.C., an American elsewhere . . .

C.d.P. This is linked to the fact that for centuries, architecture built the comfortable image of a closed and unified set and molded it. At the end of the twentieth century we witness a speeding up, the apparition of worlds, of solitary objects in the millions, countless. Pei here treats a building that is not solitary, that molds city space by cutting through it. To cut in order to bring together, to split, to create a hollowness so as to assemble the plurality of things, this is what I have always striven to do myself when presented with those segments of fragmented cities, each with their different histories and times.

P.S. Again the plurality of worlds.

C.d.P. We are witness to the proliferation of bits and pieces of cities, a proliferation happening through the growth of business and technological logics that are blind to each other. The part that is built by architects with an architectural intention represents only 10 percent of the whole. This situation is the opposite of the dream of modern architecture and urbanism that sought to replace the classical order with another world that would finally be unified, that would be a definitive unity.

P.S. That could make a world.

C.d.P. Yes, for twenty-five years they thought they were going to make a world. It is of course easy now, with hindsight, to second-guess the past. The dynamics of the time were rooted in optimism for the future, in the drifting-away of a past that had to be forgotten. The idea of remaking another world presupposed the destruction of the old one.

P.S. To warehouse it all up.

C.d.P. The blank slate, territorial conquest, military struggles, the avant-garde ahead of the masses—these are, so to speak, the figures of the style of the discourse of modernity after 1918, after the October revolution. After World War I, the Russian revolution must have been greeted with fascination, even without taking account of political affiliations. Le Corbusier, who started with a very traditional urban vision, completely changed the way he looked at cities during this period. He wrote that from then on "I will grab things by their roots." He was in no way a leftist; it was the authorities' actions in what he calls "human settlements" that interested him. He aspired to rebuild through a new economics and new techniques. He was fascinated by someone like Ford but also by the Bolshevik gesture of wiping out the past, a gesture from which was born the urbanism that changed the planet. He dreamed of replacing the world with another world, a wholly different one.

P.S. Well, there would no longer be any "whole."

C.d.P. The feeling that there was no longer a "whole" came about around the end of the sixties. And almost everywhere, the idea of a substitute world was no longer convincing. So it discreetly stopped. In France, this happened during the seventies, and since then, on the plane of urban construction, there are everywhere two cities facing and interpenetrating each other: the one that wasn't yet destroyed but had been drawn so on paper (for instance, there were plans to destroy three-fourths of Paris), and the one standing on the ruins of the old city or on beet fields. The silent stopping of modern planning, at different moments, has everywhere created hybrid situations where two worlds, two cultures, coexist in a sort of absurdity. This is the situation that has been left to us, an ensemble of found objects, the very figure Lautréamont described as the "meeting of an umbrella and a sewing machine . . ."

P.S. ". . . on a dissection table."

C.d.P. At the moment of splintering, we are forced to interpret each situation for itself, in the here and now, in its singularity. And we are still part of this double movement that consists in splitting and unifying all at once. During the epochs of the classical city, any architect could easily, by following simple rules, put a building in the city by associating it to a whole. He only needed to have a bit of culture and manners to be able to adopt the social and aesthetic codes. There were one or two great styles per century. During the period of modern urbanism, which I call Age II, there reigned also an etiquette made up of the codes of the ambient ideology that required bars and terraced roofs. Even the prewar conventional and neoclassical architects reappear after the war by drawing bars. It was only from the seventies on, and for the first time in history, that there was no longer a shared doctrine, a consensus, a common vision in how to make cities. The splintering happened then. At present, business and private interests in general overrun the processes of planning and its public institution. There is no longer an urban model that is used as reference.

Le Corbusier, Mies Van der Rohe, Alvar Aalto, and Oscar Niemeyer were the inventors of architectural forms, and they established as well a sort of grammar of the method. They left a legacy for us, a spirit, forms, and also an academism, along with glorious objects that are always heroic and isolated in principle. Their legacy includes a poetics of the heroic object but not an urban model that persisted as a universal one. Lucio Costa, at the end of his life speaking about the way he had conceived Brasília, stated in a moment of beautiful lucidity, "I wouldn't do it that way again." Basically he was saying, "We were grandiosely optimistic." And this creative and magnificent optimism troubles us for the very reason that we can understand it; we would have felt pretty much the same way during that time.

So in the end, the last century left us the figure of the isolated, heroic building. It is architecture as exception, as in your "theory of exceptions." In the midst of the general display of commercial and technical logics, we are limited to thinking only in terms of local coherence, but even this is better than the isolated building.

P.S. I call these interventions.

C.d.P. The architect comes closer to the artist's position. We are intervening in an immense jungle where the already-there is like a subject and a material. For some architects, the idea of intervention is always to create a shock, to be against, in a refusal of that which is there, in a response to the founding anticontextual gesture of modern architecture. In contrast, as the Baroque architects have shown, it is possible, from a single point in space, from a building, to read, to feel, the whole of an ensemble in a new coherence. Hence architects are no longer given the same mission as they were fifty years ago.

7. Memories/Sleep

C.d.P. A childhood memory came back to me: I am five years old; I am going to the Bourboule with my maternal grandmother. In the train at dusk, after the rain, I am looking in the direction where the sun has set over a superb, washed-over landscape. There are wooded hills and a village. I saw this landscape fragment into pieces like shadow play over a pure sky, an image that imprinted in me. When we got to the hotel, I asked for cardboard. I drew and cut up this image with the church spires, the roofs, the trees, in short, the silhouettes, and I put it in front of a lamp. My grandmother exclaimed, "But this is just what we were looking at!" It was a three-dimensional reproduction.

I had forgotten this event until recently. It brought to my mind that to draw means to set boundaries; it is as if one were designating, or naming. You enclose the bit of reality that you are perceiving and that is, for you, differentiated from the rest. It has no name but it has a contour. The contour is sufficient.

Then comes light. Phenomena are arising from the drawing that are more subtle that the contour and bring out another presence: shadows and light.

I already liked to draw when I was a little boy. Right from the start, I was very much interested in the visible. I liked to look at the world according to contours that could be cut out. I believe that a primitive language of the deaf and mute could be the outline of contours. I have described the language of words as a system of exchange: one thing is replaced by a word, then a feeling can be replaced by a word. The performance of communication, an abstraction, involves a leap from the drawing and the sign, which must have been the dominant modes of communication for thousands of years. Chinese ideographic writing is based on the image. It is a visual mode that has been systematized. It is amazing to see Japanese read a Chinese newspaper and explain that they don't know the language.

P.S. Even some Chinese can only understand each other through writing. They then write on the palm of their hands. It is one of the strangest things I have seen.

C.d.P. This kind of writing shows that, before language, there was a discourse of signs arising from this first gesture, that of drawing a line, a contour. It is said that the moment when the system of sounds and the alphabet came together was prodigious. It opened up the possibility of infinite and fast combinations, the same way that computers make it possible to store more information, to do more memorization and faster processing. The Chinese in their plural language obviously had the oral ability, but in writing, they kept the magnificent visual system of ideograms. Language itself is organized into a system to account for reality in an analytical, objective, efficient manner by allowing, even by forcing, one to free oneself from forms, from perceptions. But it cannot provide a rigorous account of the experience of vision. This distance, this radical alterity between language and the visible, is what interests me; it is basic.

For a long time drawing and language were disjointed domains for me. They came together only late. Before that, my brain was made up of two parts: one that drew and the other that named. When I wrote, it took time, I was completely immersed in it, and I neglected my projects. I wasn't able to engage in writing and drawing at the same time. It is only after I built that I was able to write and draw at the same time.

P.S. You just pointed out what happens between the oral and the written. To be at the same time in the space of the written, in the broad sense of the word, and in the image, the drawing, provokes unease.

C.d.P. When facing this, the poet is the one who requestions the naming process, who challenges lexical meaning, who rewrites language. He or she experiences anew, or makes readers re-experience and imagine, the feelings and the ideas signified by the words. Likewise, the artist challenges representation (for instance, Cézanne or Giacometti's drawings). He distances himself from the denotative image of drawing that only cuts up, designates. He reexperiences presence in a primordial manner. Literature conjures the flattening of thought, of language, that then tends to become simply a code. When I ask, "Can we think without language?" everyone seems to find this unthinkable. And yet, as I said, when I am doing architecture, an idea doesn't need to go through a statement to make it possible for me to accomplish an architectural project.

Once, just to see if it would work, I sought to put the whole of the process of a project in explicit words. It was obviously a dead end because I had to omit the thinking that happens through schemas, figures. We think with and through evocative models or drawings before we can become precise. But words are exchanged in the process. In a project, something might be called clamplike and something else threadlike because it is a way of communicating about a form, a nonidentified object. When thinking about these schemas, when doing architecture, I am also led to name, to speak. We cannot be contented with representations even though language does help to manipulate, classify, sort them. But language is secondary here.

In general, you are resistant to the idea that we can think without language.

P.S. It might be simply a question of words. I understand very well what you mean in the sense that you conceive of thought as something that is reduced by verbal communication. We can think with a language that is not necessarily that of communication. What interests me in what you just said is, first, the words "cut up," and your experience as "world traveler." Because I think that indeed, thenceforth, architecture, instead of manifesting itself in the foundations, will manifest itself increasingly as an envelopment, a gap, a way of intervening into something that is already there. We visit this something as if we were extraterrestrials or rather ultraterrestrials. We take from it a dimension that rejoins your experience as an asthmatic little boy. I too know this experience, that of trying to breathe outside of a verbal stuffing. You experienced suffocation, and with your tenacity you sought to find a new way of breathing, you started to trace a contour by trying to create a silence—to make the thing appear. You express this very well when you say that you are trying to reexperience presence. We are simply trying to free ourselves, that's all. To find, as Heidegger puts it, "a free-space in the play of time" *(Zeit-Spiel-Raum).*

C.d.P. Otherwise, there is too much.

P.S.. There is always too much. You are a sensitive guy, so you suffocate. There is too much, and there was too much.

C.d.P. There was too much in time.

P.S. Yes, there is crowding, congestion. Thus great architecture is built on an enchanted void.

C.d.P. When, in the middle of the twentieth century, modern architecture was installed in the existing city, it showed this city an iron fist, or perhaps simply a fist. This architecture had been invented to oppose the city, to take over all of its place, to substitute itself for it. Yet, it found its access limited to small pieces of it. Modern architecture at that time generally refused to engage in dialogue. It sought to appear to have come from elsewhere and claimed that surroundings are a mistake; they don't exist. Le Corbusier, at Harvard, plants his building at a slant against the whole of the urban weave. We need to realize the scope of the conceptual upheaval, the change in spatial schema that happened when the building was claimed to be an autonomous object, detached from the system of spaces, of urban empty spaces and their contours. The image of the autonomous object was born from the model of the technical object, the machine, industrialism. In a technical object, the form is dictated by the set of its own internal necessity so as to enable it to function. In the classical building, the form comes in great part from external necessities, that is, the network of empty spaces in the city that was systematized at the beginning of the sixteenth century. Thus, from the 1950s on, architectural objects engaged in a struggle against spaces, so much so that it reached the point of caricature. It is only since the 1970s that we could begin to think both of the architectural object in its autonomic state and of the space that is already there. This is what I tried to do from the start in my work. However, there is a great risk of stifling the liveliness specific to architecture and of reproducing the space that had always been there. We do need to challenge that space. You spoke of Pei's building in Washington. It is exemplary in that, instead of contradicting the classical city, it fits perfectly in it thanks to Pei giving us such a clear reading of his plan. The triangle was his opportunity. There was a time when the peak of the triangle would have led to frontality, rotundness, presence that would have given it thickness. But Pei brings in space, hollowness and light. He affirms hollowness. And in this sense, he strengthens the plan of the city of Washington. The city, which I had known only through images, when I actually saw it surprised me because of its overlarge dimensions. It is a syndrome of capital cities, and we find the same thing, for instance, in Chandigarh and in Brasília. L'Enfant, the architect who designed Washington, D.C., in the eighteenth century, thought in terms of the idea of a capital. Then he made it four times bigger, four times wider. The plan he used is found as an archetype in all the books. It is an eighteenth-century interpretation of the model of the Greek grid, a city made from a complete plan but with a monumental section. Once there, you see that the streets are very wide, more so than we would expect for streets, even for avenues, so that the buildings rise in a sort of solitude, of heaviness. We don't feel the dynamic of movement.

In order, to use your expression, for the enchanted emptiness to exist, it must be perceptible, thus maintained. If it is too big, it is no longer the same thing. Built objects then take possession, they become the magnets monopolizing all gazes.

In the monumental section of Washington, the strong presence of the buildings, each a new monument, endows them with a certain heaviness. Pei, by taking emptiness into account with his clean cuts, strongly brings back the presence of the great avenues and their light as if his building weren't there.

P.S. *As if his building weren't there . . .*

C.d.P. We can be in history, in the ancient city, and even in the one built thirty years ago, and think differently the idea of place, and this is not necessarily in the same rhetorical mode that held sway in the periods I have called Age I and Age II.

P.S. If you are like a child who is drawing, you are making tiny things, but they are immense. They are *immense* in the same way they are tiny.

C.d.P. Pei asked me to show him the tower I built in New York City, and he said, "So, that's your 'little tower,' but small dimensions become large in New York."

8. Intervention/Cézanne

C.d.P. You spoke earlier about the idea of intervention. I link this idea to something extremely important that is making its appearance today in all urban situations, namely, the return of the singular, the contingent, the unique case. The world has burst open. Most of the time the issue is not to rebuild but to intervene. The return of the particular in its guise as the outcome of a history of urbanism, art, and thinking that used to see the universal as its horizon is interesting as well as curious. It is the opposite of everything that had been predicted.

I am also thinking how this universalization and globalization, which developed in the twentieth century, were only achieved through the extreme specialization of knowledge and techniques. The journal *Tel Quel* comes to mind along with everything it represented. *Tel Quel* manifested an understanding of writing that extended into all that can be felt, thought, and seen. *Tel Quel* made me explore outside of my profession. Painting, music, literature, psychoanalysis, architecture, theory, all participated in this same movement of inquiry. This might seem evident to us, but it has to be repeated in the face of the University fragmented into self-isolated domains and the whole world divided into isolated fragments, techniques, specialties. One must make a lot of effort to reach a bit of transversality.

P.S. It is a world of separation.

C.d.P. We have the impression that there are only a few people not dwelling in separation, in specialization. It seems to me that our conversation cannot be reduced to a technical meeting between specialists, between architecture and literature, domains that moreover are foreign to each other, even though Le Corbusier raised his hat to Valéry. It seems to me that there was a turning point in the sixties. We were getting out of the first modernity, of the industrial revolution and of the vision of technical specialists devoted to efficient production. Since the sixties, we have sought another world, where there would no longer be separation between the body and consciousness, between past and future, between art and technique. It's evident in your case.

P.S. We are in a society that organizes separation. Debord dealt with this theme early on, well before 1968. It is a view shared by all those who are interested in a radical critique of society, that is, those who wish to break down the walls of separation. Many issues on urbanism cropped up at the time; an example is the International Situationists. There were attempts to abolish separation and, obviously, countermeasures taken to reorganize separation. The numerous and varied attempts at breaking the hold of separation, be they libertarian, poetic, or philosophical, have always aimed at breaking down separation in all domains, including the sexual one. But since this threatens a certain type of social organization, separation keeps coming back.

C.d.P. Separation is the method of technology, its analytical principle. It creates boundaries between fields of competence themselves aimed at resolving defined problems. No doubt, the Situationists spoke of unitarian urbanism in opposition to this separation. At the same time, probably also in opposition to the concept of separation, there was, in the works of Constant, Yona Friedman, and Georges Candilis, a flourishing of urban visions of vast and undivided systems. These architects felt that problems stemmed from separation between people, between groups, between technical objects, and between new objects that kept appearing in the thousands. And then, in new neighborhoods, there was the separation between blocks of dwellings. So these architects, in opposition to this endless division, imagined spontaneous crystal-like aggregations of cells, or large structures, forming expanses. These would be vast aboveground expanses in which all sorts of things would be installed—dwellings, stores, etc. They wanted everything linked. Theirs was the idea of a megastructure, a sort of industrialized casbah bursting with life, with encounters. A unity made up of multiplicity. Since then we have become pretty familiar with this type of space, with immense expanses or plateaus where the levels are linked to each other. These are the giant urban centers, the megamalls, the huge airports! Thence the dream crashes. Commercial reality has caught up with imaginary utopias; it is the syndrome of our time.

About intervening, you were saying that in the city there is a public space, while in literature there is none. For myself, I do think that there is one. You are intervening all the time in texts that might be fifty or two hundred years old, and you are bringing them to life, making them real. You have a unique way of getting hold of an author's body and saying, "This guy was alone in the face of everything, in the face of us, and he told us this." Without an intervention of this type at a moment, through time, forgetting reigns. Intervention brings out essential things. So what is intervening?

P.S. In other words, what is a situation or a site?

C.d.P. I spoke about the fact that, nowadays, I am more often asked to transform, to modify, an existing and overbuilt structure or neighborhood instead of constructing something new.

There is something unprecedented in this gesture. It is a curious trick history is playing; it is, so to speak, a revenge of time that forces us to approach situations case by case. After a modernity whose goal was to write the future ahead of time, to invent a future that could be planned, universalized, freed from particular cases, we find ourselves everywhere surrounded by unique situations in impossible sites. Now, there are only particular cases, contingent phenomena. This is very striking at present in the city. They say the city is global! The discourse on the global is not false. But it is often a discourse of the powers-that-be that are drawing from an ineluctable economic order. And yet, today we are surrounded by the local, the particular, these unique cases.

In art, in writing, the opposite of intervening would be what? It would be to always say: I am the first; I am wiping the slate clean; nothing existed before. I am producing an object of the beginning. This is a common attitude today. Many claim to have no roots, no master, no past. The past is crowding; the past frightens. In contrast, when you are talking about a writer or a painter or a mystic who lived three centuries or thirty years ago, it is as actual as when you write a novel or *Paradis*. You seem to respond and speak within an extremely vast field encompassing several centuries. You are not split into two sides, one the essayist and the other the novelist. Writing, building, involves reenchanting, seeing again, rereading things that are already ancient, as well as inventing things that do not yet exist. It is the same thing today in music. We are playing with time. In the space of the city, what was done two centuries ago speaks to us today. That is, if it is alive, if it hasn't been "museumified," embalmed, visited only by purchasing tickets like some neighborhoods in Europe. We have to fight for things to remain alive, modifiable. Otherwise history is put on the shelf, forgotten, left to specialists. It is no longer any kind of shared breathing space.

P.S. One wonders if someone is there.

The question of intervention is linked to the question of time. In what time are we, in what time are we living? What happened to time? You know Arthur Cravan's famous joking description of André Gide after having paid him a visit. Cravan asked him, "Monsieur Gide, what about time?" Gide pulls out his watch and says, "It's six fifteen." Obviously, Cravan wasn't inquiring about clock time. Something happened to time, to our perception of time. There are consequences in space and in all the dimensions that we might wish to evoke. I believe that this is the way we need to look at things. Since we are dealing with architecture, with cities, with constructions, with building, with inhabiting, with thinking, and since we are in a period of flight from thought (flight linked to what is in the process of happening to time), the best way to characterize a potential intervention is Heidegger's expression that I cited earlier: "a free-space in the play of time." People whose interest does not lie in time *playing* (like a child is playing) thus will tend to organize or to perpetuate the most confined spaces possible. If you need to watch for a number of global interests, you will not be able to go in the direction of creating free spaces for the play of time. Instead, if you are an artist (for instance, a writer or an architect), you would try to favor those interests by all means possible. It is the reason for which, in the question of intervention such as I am conceiving it, we enter into another temporality that is no longer that of calculation. Likewise, just as there is a politics of the city, there is a metaphysics of the city. Intervention would involve contradicting the false principle at the heart of the amnesiac piling up aimed at confining human beings.

C.d.P. In regard to temporal calculations, I evoked the ancillary towns that sprung up around Brasília, around the core plan of the city that was designed and built in four years, the perfect and pure center whose inhabitants say that it is *fechado:* closed. It is the metaphysical capital closed to the play of time. But it is no longer possible to change this immense center. Today, we can see that life is happening around it in the unplanned, nontheoretical, surrounding towns. It is there that we can imagine the future, the unplanned unknown that will give new life to the center. It is not necessarily a fantastic, visionary, exciting future, but it is a future sufficiently unknown and aleatory so as not to lock up the play of time—that's all. During the 1930s, 1940s, and 1950s, the idea of modern planning was to create a space, a city entirely under control. Thus it was closed to time, closed to the future, a city that would be finally perfect, a final solution of the city.

P.S. I would like to emphasize the expression you just used: the "final solution." It is a principle of locking up, of extermination by locking up.

C.d.P. Fairly early on during the sixties, some people realized that modern urbanism was oppressive, totalitarian. Constant's and Friedman's projects, which I mentioned earlier, are utopias rooted in the idea of a city that would have time in its future, that would not be closed, that would keep going. The idea of a work that remains open kept coming back all through the sixties (something that was described by Umberto Eco). Of course, in the urbanism of that time there were still technical megastructures lacking in flexibility. These megastructures remained ideas of planning impervious to chance. The neighborhood of La Défense in Paris, for instance, is also a complex megastructure, a giant parking facility serving the city. But the notion of work in progress can count on the future.

P.S. James Joyce's "work in progress [in English in French text]" makes its appearance in terms of verbalization, which reminds me that *Paradis,* too, involves a "work in progress." Regarding the notion of intervention, I would like to bring up again both Pei and yourself. It seems to me that, in contrast to an architectural vision of piling things up, intervention consists in cutting out excess so as to produce an effect of empty space, a sharp, empty blade. Something that would resemble the disengagement of what Heidegger called "free space."

C.d.P. Yes, exactly, it involves creating a new situation by cutting and recutting, opening, giving breathing room—that's the ideal. The city must be able to be a planned free territory, and there must be a plan that is open to uncertainty. There was a milestone in urban vision around 1550. At that time there appeared the notion that it was possible to draw from active emptiness. Cities were organized according to major plans conceived on the basis of empty spaces. This was the appearance of the Baroque in the cities. In this view, the building was no longer the only center for the gaze. The built was linked to a vast spatial system. In contrast, four centuries later, the moment appears when any building work, any city comes to be built through the addition of objects in an accumulation of uncertainty. The numbers are occasionally planned but the substance is escaping. The notion of intervention cutting through excess involves revising this incredible accumulation of innumerable objects. So how are we to understand this intervention?

P.S. For Heidegger, free space is linked to *Gelassenheit,* which translates as "serenity," "letting go," which is said to mean evenness of soul in the face of things and a spirit open to secrets. Very strangely, this free space makes us aware of proximity, makes us notice that which is very near and so is often neglected. Thenceforth, the time in which we are is quadridimensional; it includes the past, the present, and the future as well as a fourth dimension that comes first and encompasses the other three. That is something fundamental to which we need to accede in order to gain a knowledge that has never transpired in the history of metaphysics.

C.d.P. So, you would call the fourth . . .

P.S. Time, inasmuch as it gives us past, present, and future. We can well see that this is in opposition to obliteration, "museumification," the excessive commemoration of the past, the rush into the present, and the absence of a new future inasmuch as it is present, almost visible, everywhere. We are dwelling in increasingly virtual sites.

C.d.P. This fourth dimension that enables us to escape to the present version of a time consciousness stuck in the technical mode . . .

P.S. . . . in the market . . .

C.d.P. . . . yes, the market, technology, where time is reduced to a sole vector defined by progress. Today, there is a past that is eliminated, ridiculed, or "museumified" at the same time it is forgotten because it is no longer actual, and there is a present that is simply action oriented. As to the future, it has been turned into an increasingly closer horizon. The decision makers' future cannot go beyond returns on investments, beyond what can be planned to make money. You mention that it is from the moment the earth was entirely known and accessible, and later with the end of the major political blocs of the cold war, that time has thus been reduced, frozen. When we no longer had a spatial elsewhere on the planet, there was no longer a temporal elsewhere—no more utopia. But your quadridimensional time is our consciousness, and it is a time that encompasses the past and could not exist without the consciousness of the future.

P.S. It is the reason why the problem of the bursting forth of an encompassing force—that's what I call it, an encompassing subject-force—is by nature pro-infinite and can transform our days' presence. My *Paradis,* continuous, discontinuous, is nothing else but this encompassing intervention force, a crack into the closure of time, space, and language. Could someone give an account of it? That someone's question seems to me absolutely decisive on the political as well as the metaphysical plane. I mentioned Pei and the museum he built in Washington, D.C. This museum is arriving, it is destroying without destroying all that surrounds it, and what surrounds us is the Library of Congress with its nineteenth-century-style kitsch that makes us laugh when we see what has been painted inside its cupolas, namely, the completely false representations of history in the style of Puvis de Chavanne. Intervention is thus *historial* in nature rather than historical because of this breach in time. I find it interesting that this was created by a Chinese-American architect. I mentioned this Washington museum, the bank tower in Hong Kong that is Pei's sort of personal revenge on his father who was a banker, the concert hall in Dallas, the Louvre pyramids. That's what I call intervening in an engaged situation, forcing it to disgorge. I believe that you are attempting the same thing in your Cité de la Musique, your sequentially colored Tokyo tower, your New York tower, your project for Luxembourg, etc. These are absolving gestures. They are not protests, they are not desires to produce something new; rather, these gestures are almost exorcisms. I am using very heavy words here. In the face of space possessed by the confining of time, itself given up to computation, an intervention, whether it be with language or with architecture, would consist of freeing what can be freed. This would occur right on the spot you happen to be in, at the moment you are there. In a way, Pei liberated the Louvre. He has also "liberated" Washington from its nineteenth-century weight.

C.d.P. I am coming back to the gesture of absolution, to intervention in quest of the times, future and past, in a space. In the West, during the last century the concern was to find the universal formula, to map absolute space so as to rebuild from the bottom up, to definitely eliminate the issue of individual cases and alienation.

P.S. Yes, yes, and that is also a political question.

C.d.P. Marx and Lenin come to mind, but the same sort of vision also came from Taylorism, Fordism, from the type of industrial organization influencing ways of thinking after World War I. At that time, Le Corbusier began to think his urbanism method in terms of a city of one million people, with the idea of a city built from nothing and without all the classical and picturesque points of reference that had marked his growing-up years. He was clearly as much under the spell of the radical blank slate approach of the 1918 Russian revolution as he was fascinated by American industrial methods. He was struck by automation, aviation, advances in mass warfare, and computations. He was fascinated by large numbers, by any organization capable of dealing with human beings in large quantities. The technical project was advancing by leaps and bounds through military research—this was called total war. Today, the idea is to wage a zero-deaths war. After World War I, there might have been the realization of a new time, one haunted by the powerlessness of the soldier facing the machine, of the heroic and suffering individual, the one to whom Céline was to give voice. The discourse of progress was to resolve the issue, to seek universal solutions in order to end the always uncontrollable drama of the particular.

Thus, in the course of the last half of the twentieth century, there was an obsession with dealing with masses in terms of production, distribution, the city, population growth, and rural exodus. That was industry. And then, numbers stopped getting bigger and became abstract. That's the computer. We are no longer forced to think in terms of series, of the universal, of making things uniform, because it is now possible to deal with the particular, to atomize it, to store it in memory. Thence, the advent of the individual as consumer: that's the passage we have lived through.

P.S. So now the camera is inside our heads even when it is exteriorized through the cameras of general police surveillance. It is also in the heads of writers, architects, cultural promoters, and financiers. This is the advent of the era of the absolute subjectivity of an internalized camera. This involves racing toward a senselessness that goes well beyond the issue of knowing whether the world is absurd or if humanism still has something to tell us about this adventure. Unless you have a very sharp metaphysical viewpoint, there is nothing you can say to match this out-of-bounds excess. That's why I am defending the question of a preexisting infinite from which we draw the finite. *Paradis* is a book that is "infinitist," from which I can bring out various interventions in time and in space, since I can recite it everywhere and in any situation in order to show that language passes through everything. The fact of passing *through* defines the idea of intervention, of cutting. It is not the same attitude as that of being in the service of a collectivity that has been reduced to its finiteness in order to be exploited as such. If everything is social, for instance, or if everything is sexual, I would have very few chances of being able to intervene from the outside. I would be told constantly that my intervention doesn't mesh with the "previously judged," that is, with the unification that the market presupposes, with its voluntary servitude, or as Debord puts it even better, with "the overworked salaried of the void." I stress that "nothing is sharper than the point of the infinite." I will ask myself, when facing any spatial event, whether it includes a dimension of infinity, whether, for instance, a particular architect gives me the impression that she or he has meditated about this or about emptiness. If not, I will not feel comfortable in that space since, one way or another, the architect has not been able to ensure the passage of the "sharp point" of time. In this regard, Baudelaire asks an architect's question when he wonders why the spectacle of the sea is so infinitely, eternally pleasant. He responds by saying that it is because the sea offers at once the idea of immensity and of movement, "six or seven miles (the unity of total infinity)." We are already in the realm of allegory, that is, the possibility of suggesting the idea of the total infinite through some sort of form or building in space. Let me give it to you in a diminutive form, in this case, a Chinese one. When we are looking at a Chinese painting of a landscape, whether it be mountains or rocks, there is always a small cabin in a corner with the silhouette of an almost invisible person, and we know he is the one who painted that particular roll.

C.d.P. A parallel image comes to mind, that of the island. This might be an equivalent of your notion of an infinite diminutive. I was thinking about this in regard to an urbanism project that I did in Manhattan. I perceived the Manhattan grid, the urban weft of the streets, as an immense infinite oratorio. It spread without discontinuity. It should be seen as something like your fourth temporal dimension. It persists and continues. It is inflexible but it opens up freedom. It is law, and yet it doesn't stop rivers: it reveals them. It makes a sharp stop at their shore. The grid is present all the way to the edges without any other thing because it has no end. This infinite is manifested by precise sensations: streets of almost Gothic proportions, emptiness of light and sky coming down all the way to the asphalt—emptiness sculpted by the stop made up of the glass and stone of the facades and, at the end, still the light, the water, the river, the shore, and again the sky, higher. That's precisely where the infinite resides. It came from far away. It could keep going endlessly. It is the sea that has intervened, that has stopped it, or rather it is the rivers. Manhattan is an absolute boat, a fixed one. This makes me also think of *Paradis,* where a window frame of the Café Beaubourg reveals, by sharply cutting into it, the notion of a text that runs, that has begun and that will continue, and that your reader's own moment of reading will stop.

P.S. The abolition of separation, breaking it open . . .

C.d.P. Breaking open the text in the window just as a passerby would. There is an infinite sentence in *Paradis* that seems to be the opposite of versification and seems to me to be playing in the same register in a new way. By transforming the sentence, it breaks the structural, functional, and chronological relationship with language. The continuous text yields the necessity of a different reading. It is no longer a sentence that delivers the message but one that liberates the word, precisely just as the song, as psalmody, does. The words seem to be set free. There you are asking the question of a rhythmic form. "I declared words to be free, equals" (Hugo). The word is an entity that is bursting out. This can be heard in rap music. Its grammar can be fuzzy; it can be interpreted differently from one line to the next. In *Paradis* I see a plane of language on which you seem to focus and that comes to you through tropisms. It is a personal plane; it is not a lexicon but already an underlying thought. The word is already the idea. I heard something identical when you spoke about Claudel and how his language is creating his extremely sharp "organ of perception." Language is an eye, an ear, a sense of smell . . .

P.S. . . . the five senses . . .

C.d.P. . . . through which objects are constantly signaling to you. It is thought, perception in motion. An architect too must navigate in this sort of intertext.

P.S. In an interspace.

C.d.P. That's it, and one that creates figures, experiences, memories, surprises, and wonder, but also suffocation, uneasiness, and absurdity needing correction. The past can be heavy, so its weight sometimes tempts us to forget everything that was before, but this past also makes it possible to see, to interpret, to understand, to act. Architects have their points of intimate contact with art, cities, the history of representation, geometrical drawings and axonometric projections, medieval representations, the nude, open spaces, or again with the appearance of perspective, with the Cézanne moment, and with the automobile, the plane, with motion—that is, with the means through which we can think the visible. This seems to be a crazy universe, disorganized, powerful. And yet, I am beginning to feel, to admit, that there is not, after all, a consciousness outside of language. There is a presence of language. I was thinking about this yesterday, and that is what our conversations are bringing out for me. In order for it to be thinking about space, for it to be perception of the notion of emptiness between things, and for the consciousness of this notion to exist, words have to be spoken, words have to exist within a layer of correlates, a sort of site of language. Without words, this isolation of the phenomenon of space could not have existed as such in perception; so much matter, so many of the objects surrounding us, seem to be the only ones existing and polarizing sensations and practice. Likewise, this holds as well for Lao Tzu's statement I mentioned earlier in that it opens up the notion of emptiness and makes it sensible to the consciousness of listeners who couldn't perceive it before. Lao Tzu's statement is longer than the word "space"; it is not abstract but rather has some of the characteristics of an ideogram. But it is language nonetheless. And it is thanks to Lao Tzu's statement that, after my lectures, many people came to tell me: "I understood."

Language might be the precondition for consciousness, for any kind of perception. Is that true? Light on this issue might be shed by looking at the research done on individuals suffering from hypervisual or hyperauditive autism. I found keys for this issue of perception thinking in your writings about Cézanne through a different reading of your text in your book, *L'éloge de l'infini*,[1] this without the very telling illustrations that you had chosen. You are the first to point out that Cézanne had very interesting things to say. In your text, we can hear Cézanne's lucid awareness that he was in the process of establishing another mode of the gaze, another status of the visible. In fact, from the beginning, the whole of the question of space has focused around the issue of its representation such as depth, perspective, etc. Cézanne had a great impact on me. He was there before architecture.

P.S. Cézanne *was* an architect.

C.d.P. You bring out how his language seemed necessary to him. He was in a skiff of sensations where he needed his internal monologue, his few sentences, as if they were oars, so as to keep on moving, to remember that he was in a skiff, that he had a unique point of view, that the landscape he was looking at was not reality and only existed in his personal vision. Did the artist know this? Cézanne knew everything. Thus, in your text, in between language and space, I understand Cézanne as seeker of his space. The text is formidable. Language might indeed be the condition for thinking space. The world had to be named for it to be seen. The seed for the whole of the notion of modern space in painting and architecture lies here. Cézanne wasn't quite saying this because for him "it is all a matter of sensations," but the words are there, and thanks to him new things will be named by others, thus perhaps felt in the future. Cézanne no longer wanted to draw like Ingres. He wanted to structure a new space in which there were no longer lines and values. You chose the paintings where this can best be seen. Emptiness and fullness have the same pull, the same presence. Sky and earth are also strong. Without words, he would not know this.

P.S. And as Cézanne himself said: "When I went to see Zola (his close childhood friend), I found only people who were talking about their royalties. I tried to talk about Baudelaire, but no one was interested." Cézanne was a great reader of Baudelaire. It is this relationship to poetry and to thought, thus also to the visible, thus to space and to time, to which I tried to do justice and that explains why a work is worth so much while nobody really knows how it was made and what it is speaking about. Money always takes the place of that which we don't understand but which we sense is very important, dangerous, anguishing. From there, one goes to Picasso or to Bacon. All these painters were saying things to which not enough thought is given. "It is of no import if this diminutive infinite is sufficient to suggest the idea of the total infinite," says Baudelaire. I believe that one can say this about Cézanne's paintings. And Baudelaire adds, "Twelve or fourteen miles of liquid in motion are enough to give the highest idea of beauty offered to man on his transient shelter." I am thinking again about what you were saying about Manhattan, where water and sky take on a particularly impressive form. However, the fact of suggesting the immensity and the motion, wherever they may be, in the mountain, the countryside, or a city neighborhood, seems to me to be the same thing. The sea doesn't have to be on the street corner. It can be here, instantly, if I conjure it. Instantly, you have memories or desires of the sea. It is very beautiful to have an evocation of the infinite while we are in a transient shelter, a *habitacle*.[2] And what would such a *habitacle* be? The word designates the cockpit of a plane as well as the glass-enclosed binnacle of a ship containing instruments of navigation. Thence, we are linked to something that can be measured.

C.d.P. But then we also need the immeasurable. We must be able to convoke the sea, as you say, from that *habitacle.* I have in front of me a passage of yours: "Let us gaze at the urban landscape in which we are thenceforth locked in. It is an accumulation of superimposed and even mobile boxes. Here corporeal separation provides the stage for isolation. The place where we will end, the cemetery, brings this sort of organization to its culmination."

P.S. To come back to intervention and breaches in relation to their opposite, locking up, there is another dimension in *Paradis* that is never, or almost never, noticed and that is essentially biblical. The Hebrew text has been translated countless times. It is an extraordinary market. You have Bibles everywhere, including in the drawers of Anglo-Saxon hotels. You have the King James version in English and Luther's version in German. There has never been an important canonical version of the Bible in French. That is why someone had to undertake making biblical scansion be heard in French. That work is called *Paradis.* The book involves a reminder of prophetic forms in which aggression toward nations, or the faithfulness of a people to its God, is manifested through language, its name, its words, and its written revelation. The Bible disturbs on account of its infinite character. There is no end in it. The absence of punctuation shifts weight to accentuation. The fact of saying something, of engaging oneself into this chanted flux called "psalms," is guided by accentuation, by mouth, by tasting. We could call the Bible the war of taste. It seems to me that, in the context of the time, Cézanne's strange religious law was symptomatic. It is as if he were introducing the divine in every little thing. It is for this reason that he didn't get along with Zola or with Clemenceau, whose portrait he refused to paint. We know that he was reticent by nature: "These people are up to no good!" He claimed obsessively that he had always been afraid of being entrapped. *Trapped*. He was afraid of being touched. He preferred to keep his distance. And yet, Cézanne was the one who intervened to abolish separation. He rejected separated representation. He wanted everything at once and claimed to speak truth in painting. In reality, this corresponded to his fundamental eroticism.

I think that we need to introduce Eros in our discussion since, just as the word, architecture too was to be more or less sensual, erotic, more or less disposed to procure a sensation of diminutive infinite—which, as usual, will also be a political intervention.

C.d.P. Cézanne said that this will come to pass through color. For him, perfect and descriptive lines in Ingres's style do not count, and neither do modeled values or depictions in the round. On the contrary, he succeeds in making emptiness and fullness into equivalent substances that are not separated but are communicating with each other. He was the first to want to paint this, or at any rate to be aware of it, to see it. He breaks through the polarization of the object.

Would you say that *Paradis* establishes a relationship of the present moment, of the syllable, of accentuation, with the sensation of immensity, or rather of the infinite? Pollock also comes to mind here.

P.S. At any rate, it is the opposite of the process of human "massification" tied to a state of constant recording, albeit with access only to a limited number of words and thus producing what I call drivel.

C.d.P. Recently, I got a twenty-page fax, and all the pages were covered with formulas. I didn't know what it was, but I was told that the formulas corresponded to a numerical image that, by mistake, had been printed in characters instead. Numeration might even be the Mona Lisa! It is interesting, this visualization of data storage and the performance of numerical memorization that enables an infinite conservation in a binary alphabet mode. We are living a parallel mutation, perhaps even a reduction of language, of the role of experience itself.

P.S. Thus of the body.

C.d.P. *Paradis,* for instance, could be read as the antithesis of all that. A record of inner experience.

P.S. It's an escape. I very much like the energy of escaping. It makes me think of Casanova who was writing in his cell at the Plombs, in Venice, with a nail dipped in jam. This was to yield eventually three thousand pages. There is also an aphorism by Lichtenberg: "There are very few things that we can taste with all of our five senses at once." I believe that Cézanne did want us to taste his paintings with all five senses at once. I believe that Picasso did the same thing with his collages by introducing guitars, fragments of music, bits of newspaper clippings. We would need to expand on how citations, collages, and montages have become necessary for opening up this free space of time. Citing is also a very ancient art of Hebrew civilization. As for me, I say that these are not citations but *proofs.* Historical proofs.

C.d.P. I like your bringing together citations and collages. I would also see this in terms of the city, but in an inverted manner. Intervening means cutting through an ensemble of collages, of citations. It is the same gesture whether looking for one or the other. You are installing a context, an epoch that reveals our own to us.

P.S. Walter Benjamin, whom I like a lot, made the following magnificent statement about citations: "Citations, in my work, are like highway robbers suddenly appearing fully armed and robbing the passerby of his convictions."

C.d.P. "Suddenly appearing," that's it. You cite Cézanne: "There should not be too many lines, because too many lines is the same as writing with too many 'as ifs [comme],'" but sensations just suddenly appear.

P.S. Of course. One eliminates the "as if." Rimbaud never used "as if."

C.d.P. Cézanne sees the world in a way that makes everything present at once. He said that lines don't count, but rather truth lies in colors, and that they have the same intensity whether they represent an apple, a sky, or leaves. They only have different rhythmic states.

P.S. He calls this having a grasp of his *motif.*[3]

C.d.P. We get the impression that he felt at first that he was not very good at drawing but that he had a formidable gaze. He guessed that this was his luck. His hand was never to be able to short-circuit his thought. He had to meditate on the means. The time he spent in the Louvre made him understand that it is not through the line that it is happening. So, are people going to understand? Because there are indeed lines in Cézanne! And yet, he said that it must not pass through the lines. He no longer looked at the line as drawing, as the blocking out of an object by a faithful hand, but rather as a direction of space, as the primary line of vision. This can be seen in his watercolors, in color fields engendering and creating zones of passage from one state to another. Line is made of color, and it is the locus of transformation, of passage.

P.S. And above all, it is endless. This is extraordinarily blasphemous in terms of all preceding metaphysics.

C.d.P. In order to give all, one mustn't take all. One must suspend. You cite a wonderful account reported by Gasquet of Cézanne invoking Balzac's novel, *The Wild Ass's Skin:* "During the whole of my youth, I wanted to paint this," and Cézanne then proceeded to read the description of a white tablecloth, "white like newly fallen snow on which arose symmetrically the dinner dishes and flatware crowned by blond rolls." And he adds: "I am now aware that I should only want to paint that on which 'arose symmetrically the dinner dishes and flatware' and the 'blond rolls,' but if I paint 'crowned,' I am in trouble. And if I do really put my plates and flatware and my rolls in equilibrium like they are in nature, you can be certain that crowns, snow, and all the rest shall all be there."

P.S. It's the diminutive infinite. You paint a diminutive infinite and the rest will be there.

C.d.P. Your citations from Cézanne are very strong. We can see him as a silent, solitary figure serenely suffering with absolute self-confidence. It is not a "doomed artist" who suffered.

P.S. Neither was Picasso.

C.d.P. Picasso had self-doubts but also a constant awareness of his genius. At any rate, he was always doing battle. You show Cézanne happy and well aware of the repercussions he might have in the next century. You are citing him again in his plenitude when he says that it is enough for him to be alone in his sensations to be happy.

P.S. "Sensations are at the base of what I am doing, so I think I am impenetrable." That is very deep.

C.d.P. And he was the first to say that he was not transcribing nature. Painting is another nature. It is a parallel world that is something else. This was not what the Impressionists were saying. Sensations came from Cézanne himself: they were him. Nature was a permanent pretext that he had to penetrate, but what he was painting was not nature. He was conscious of the entities that are nature and the whole of the canvas. They are different entities altogether. So he turned the idea of representation upside down. He put himself first. He was a phenomenologist. The world is not what we are perceiving. We are submitting it to our perceptions. The Impressionists had prepared the ground, but he turned upside down the idea of representation that had existed since the Renaissance.

P.S. "We must usurp power," said Picasso about nature. What Picasso said about Bonnard is awful: "Bonnard was so preoccupied by nature that he wanted to correct his paintings. He was adding a bit more pink—a potpourri of indecisions."

As for me, without any transition, I would like to make the apology of sleep. I find that Cézanne's paintings sleep in an admirable manner. Great works of art sleep powerfully, and I would gladly invent for myself a sort of trade in this society that is increasingly crazy with absolute subjectivity: that of sleeper.

I believe that this can be interesting to you as an architect because I am volunteering to be a sleeper of museums, a sleeper of paintings. I could also be a sleeper of cathedrals, of basilicas, of concert halls, of theaters, of gardens, etc., a sleeper of cities. An architect is someone who will tell me in an entirely new way what a room is, or a hallway, a staircase, a bathroom, a living room, what we used to call a dining room, and don't forget the toilet. About toilets, I want to cite Bacon, because it is he who introduced sinks, vomiting, and latrines into the history of painting. And then a street, a neighborhood, an unexpected bay, water, light, the sky—something that *sleeps* well. That sleeps beyond the spectacle, so as to find again time lost, things past. Proust's *Remembrance of Things Past*[4] begins with sleep. And yet there's nothing more *awake,* more lucid. Proust was a great architect, he starts from his bed.

Afterword: For the Musicians!

Dear Christian de Portzamparc,

Dreaming about your Cité de la Musique, I imagine that finally there will be a place of movement, open even under the ground, where the fulgurant sensation (I just experienced it again a short while ago when waking up) that we are born of sound so as to return to the evanescing of vibration orchestrated in space. Music is sacred, of course, because from all sides it attempts to evoke this point, this band or ribbon, this impalpable knot. In the depth of sleep: a quick figure of eight, barely apprehended by the human passerby, but at the same time unforgettable, and which colors his all-too-heavy journey, its architecture never free enough. I like your project. I can already hear it. It will be a great event for Paris (and the whole of France), a Paris finally coming out of its nineteen-century deafness, which itself came about when the Baroque was brought to a stop, something we once talked about, you remember, with passion. What pleases me, in our dialogue, is that it is really turned toward music; you have geometry and the lightness of matter, and I, syllables and words. I would like to read *Paradis* in your City in the city. Simply a mouth, a throat, lungs, accentuation, diction, so as, in one spot, to bring to life the thought realized into curves. And then there would be a concert. Bodies dancing. And then, gradually, like in an atomic reactor, the rest would follow.

Your project is itself a partition. Nothing in it is declamatory, closed, oppressive. It is a footbridge, a summoner of unities, transparence. It is indeed a "folly," in the desirable eighteenth-century sense of the word, a calm, melodic, happy folly, rediscovered through the East. I see the trees and the water; I am in a room communicating through propagation with all other rooms; people are talking, playing, quiet, jumping, looking at the sky, dwelling in the silence. Thence, the city needs this more than anything, this being turned upside down, defended against itself, the dead allowed to escape—we are living in the ear, the decision maker of everything.

As Mozart wrote from Milan to his sister: "Above us, there is a violinist, below, another, next door, a singing teacher giving lessons, and in the last room, across from ours, an oboist. This makes composing fun! It gives me ideas."

I was thinking about this these last few days: so, the only dedication I would like to make for everything that I have written would be the following: "For the musicians!" Yes, for the musicians, only for them. I can see that we are in agreement.

With friendship,

Philippe Sollers
May 1986

Notes

The translator gives heartfelt thanks to Alexandre Vital for his help in resolving some complex translation conundrums, to Deborah Hauptmann for her insightful contributions to the translation, and to Nancy Sauro for her fine copyediting of the manuscript.

1. Destruction

1. ["Money" and "towers" are in English in the French text.— *Trans.*]

2. André S. Labarthes, writer and director, "Philippe Sollers, l'isolé absolu" (1998), television series *Un siècle d'écrivains*.

3. Étienne-Louis Boullée, a great French Utopian architect (1728–1799).

4. [Sollers's choice of the word "beautiful" to characterize images of violence might be thought objectionable. However, there is a usage in both French and English in which "beautiful" can refer to the uniqueness and/or exemplarity of a phenomenon (see *Trésor de la langue française informatisé* at http://atilf.atilf.fr/, and *Webster's Third New International Dictionary*). Sollers's use of the word could also be interpreted to refer to the enduring emotional aesthetic effect carried by the images. Picasso's *Guernica* comes to mind as an example. It is beautiful in that it succeeds in conveying, through aesthetic means, an enduring representation of the agony suffered by the

victims of war. Another factor in Sollers's choice of words might be the influence of ancient Greek philosophy that conceived of truth and beauty as equivalent. In that sense, Sollers could see the images of the attacks on the towers as "beautiful" in that they stand for the truth of the event.—*Trans.*]

5. ["Trading" is in English in the French text.—*Trans.*]

2. Can We Think without Language?

1. [In his writing on cities, de Portzamparc has formulated what he refers to as Age I, Age II, and Age III of the city. To the first he offers the attributes of foundations and consolidations, sedimentary cities founded on geometries and universal orders, dense, intensive, intact (ancient). Age II was marked by substitution as opposed to foundations, based on the principle of the tabula rasa, or the principle of eradication. These cities were expansive and homogeneous; they have often been termed "visionary" (modern). Age III of the city he sees as beginning with the ending of the postwar housing crisis. It is "protean," "multiform"; it is metamorphic and heterogeneous, in other words, nonnumeric, constituted in the multiplicity of One. It is in Age III of the city that the implications of "intervention," of the "case by case" will be seen.—*Deborah Hauptmann*]

2. Philippe Sollers, *Le Paradis de Cézanne* (Paris: Gallimard, 1995), 34–36.

3. [There is a wordplay in the original: in French *cartes* means "cards" as in a card game and also "maps." And Descartes could be translated as "cards" or "maps," or "some maps" in English.—*Trans.*]

4. [Sollers, *Le Paradis de Cézanne,* 94–98.—*Trans.*]

5. [Jean François Champollion was a nineteenth-century Egyptologist who first deciphered hieroglyphs with the help of the three texts on the Rosetta stone.—*Trans.*]

6. ["Was heist denken?" is the title Heidegger gave to a 1951–52 lecture course that was subsequently published under the same title in 1954 (Tübingen: Max Niemeyer Verlag, 1–8, 48–52, and 79–86). The lectures were divided into two parts; in English they have been translated as "what is called thinking" and "what calls for thinking." We see this exactly reflected in Sollers's comment. However, it should be noted that while the early English translation of this text by Fred D. Wieck and J. Glenn Gray (New York: Harper & Row, 1968, 3–18, 113–21) interpreted the title literally as "what is called thinking," later versions tended to correct this misconception (as Sollers similarly suggests) by translating the title of the paper as "what calls for think-

ing." For example, see Martin Heidegger, *Basic Writings,* ed. David Farrell Krell (London: Routledge, 1978).—*Deborah Hauptmann*]

7. [Quoted in Heidegger, *What Is Called Thinking?* trans. Wieck and Gray, 93.—*Trans.*]

8. [Emile Zola, *The Masterpiece,* trans. Thomas Walton and Roger Pearson (Oxford: Oxford University Press, 1999).—*Trans.*]

9. [In English usually referred to as "The Large Bathers" or "Nudes in a Landscape."—*Trans.*]

10. Christian de Portzamparc, *Généalogie de la forme / Genealogy of Forms,* bilingual ed., English translation by Stephen Wright (Paris: Dis Voir, 1996).

11. [Ibid., 23.—*Trans.*]

12. [Ibid.—*Trans.*]

13. [Ibid.—*Trans.*]

14. [Ibid., 63.—*Trans.*]

15. [Arthur Rimbaud, "Vowels," in *Rimbaud Complete,* trans. Wyatt Mason (New York: Modern Library / Random House, 2002), 104.—*Trans.*]

16. [These are of course French vowels.—*Trans.*]

17. [Arthur Rimbaud, *A Season in Hell; Illuminations,* trans. Enid Rhodes Peschel (New York: Oxford University Press, 1973), 141–43.—*Trans.*]

18. [Arthur Rimbaud, "Villes," in *Illuminations* (Paris: Gallimard, 1972), 137–38; *Illuminations,* trans. Louise Varèse (New York: New Directions Books, 1957), 61–63.—*Trans.*]

19. *Correspondence between Goethe and Schiller, 1794—1805,* trans. Liselotte Dieckmann (New York: Peter Lang, 1994), 207. From the letter to Schiller, 14 August 1797: "Yesterday I saw a performance of the opera Palmira. Above all I had the pleasure of seeing one part in perfection, namely the decorations. The great difficulty with theater-architecture is that one has to understand the principles of real architecture, and yet has to deviate from them according to the present purpose. Architecture in a higher sense is supposed to express a high, serious, solid existence. It can hardly allow itself to be charming without becoming weak."

20. [French and North African shanty towns. The reference is to *bidon,* "oil drum," one of the materials from which the dwellings were made.—*Trans.*]

21. [François Jullien, *A Treatise on Efficacity: Between Western and Chinese Thinking,* trans. Janet Lloyd (Honolulu: University of Hawai'i Press, 2004).—*Trans.*]

22. [Le Corbusier, *The Radiant City*, trans. Pamela Knight, Eleanor Levieux, and Derek Coltman (London: Faber and Faber, 1967).—*Trans.*]

23. [French public housing.—*Trans.*]

24. [de Portzamparc, *Généalogie de la forme / Genealogy of Forms*, 85.—*Trans.*]

25. [Ibid.—*Trans.*]

26. [Arthur Rimbaud, "La Pléiade," in *Oeuvres Complètes* (Paris: Gallimard, 1972), 251–52; Wyatt Mason, ed. and tr., *I Promise to Be Good: The Letters of Arthur Rimbaud* (New York: Modern Library, 2003), 30.—*Trans.*]

27. [Ibid., 32–33.—*Trans.*]

28. Ibid., 33; emphases in original.

3. The Power of Dreams

1. [The Louis Vuitton-Moët Hennessy Tower in Manhattan.—*Trans.*]

2. Dream (1969 or 1970), premonition of the water tower: At the base there were heather and big stones that were in my way at times. I had probably awakened some time earlier, and I had just moved the blanket and gone to find a pen and drawing paper. The forest was sparse. In this end of the night, humidity and light blended (as in a birth). One could guess the dawn sky beyond the trees, of a vaporization of light mounting from the ground, slow and frozen in space. But there was this zone of electric light that was giving me back to the night. One of the segments of the big building against which I had fallen asleep was lit and was projecting on the brush, and on the ground was a yellow puddle in which all the atmosphere of the evening found refuge. With it, I could still believe in the night. I then understood (as I had partly woken up) the polygonal and regular composition of this construction, probably opened on each of its faces with tall glass doors, like the one I had in front me. (I knew it) I thought that I wasn't going to be able to sleep any longer, and this led me to look for drawing paper, but there wasn't enough light.

3. [Philippe Sollers, *Passion fixe* (Paris: Gallimard, 2000).—*Trans.*]

4. [Martin Heidegger, *Poetry, Language, Thought,* trans. and introduction by Albert Hofstadter (New York: Harper & Row, 1971), 181. Other terms Heidegger uses to define a thing are "particular," "material," "near, at hand," "narrow, immediate," and "a thing-for-itself." Objects, in the sense of "objectified," are neither distant nor near.

See also Heidegger, *What Is a Thing?* trans. W. B. Barton Jr. and Vera Deutsch (Chicago: Hery Regnery, 1967).—*Trans.*]

5. [Heidegger, *Poetry, Language, Thought,* trans. Hofstadter, 182. Heidegger discusses the Old German etymology of "thing" as a gathering, bringing together. The French quote used by Sollers uses "Things, each gathering." I have kept Hofstadter's translation and his invented word "thinging."—*Trans.*]

6. [Ibid. The Hofstadter translation has: "Only that which modestly is born from the world and through it, will become one day a thing."—*Trans.*]

7. [Arthur Rimbaud, *Illuminations,* La Pléiade Series (Paris: Gallimard, 1972). English quotes from Arthur Rimbaud, *A Season in Hell; The Illuminations,* trans. Enid Rhodes Peschel (London: Oxford University Press, 1973), 140–41.—*Trans.*]

8. Arthur Rimbaud, "After the Flood," in *Poésie,* La Pléiade Series (Paris: Gallimard 1972), 121. English quote from Rimbaud, *A Season in Hell; Illuminations,* trans. Peschel, 109–11.—*Trans.*]

9. [From the poem "Movement," in *A Season in Hell; Illuminations,* trans. Peschel, 163.—*Trans.*]

10. [A spectacular tall building constructed in the shape of an ark in Paris in 1989.—*Trans.*]

4. *Passion fixe*

1. [Philippe Sollers, *Passion fixe* (Obsession) (Paris: Gallimard, 2000).—*Trans.*]

2. [Philippe Sollers, *Women,* trans. Barbara Bray (New York: University of Columbia Press, 1992).—*Trans.*]

3. Philippe Sollers, *Paradis* (Paris: Seuil, 1981).

4. Sollers, *Women,* trans. Bray.

5. [Lautréamont is the pseudonym of Isidore-Lucien Ducasse.—*Trans.*]

6. Philippe Sollers, "Folio," in *Visions à New-York* (Paris: Gallimard, 1998).

5. "Manufacturability"

The authors coin the word *fabricabilité* to mean the property that allows something to be made and/or manufactured. I have rendered this with "manufacturablility," whose meaning will become clearer in the discussion.

1. Martin Heidegger, "The Question concerning Technology," in *Basic Writings,* ed. David Farrell Krell (London: Routledge, 1978), 320–22.

2. ["Voici le soir charmant ami du criminel." Charles Baudelaire, *Les Fleurs du Mal (The Flowers of Evil),* bilingual edition, trans. Richard Howard (Boston: David R. Godine, 1982), 99.—*Trans.*]

3. [Guy Debord, *Panegyric,* trans. James Brook (London: Verso, 1991), 76–77.—*Trans.*]

4. [Guy Debord, *Society of the Spectacle,* trans. anonymous (Detroit: Black and Red, 1977).—*Trans.*]

5. [Aragon, *Paris Peasant,* trans. Simon Watson Taylor (Boston: Exact Change, 1994)—*Trans.*]

6. [Constant Nieuwenhuis (1920–2005), Dutch artist, most noted for his utopian works of urbanism and architecture known as New Babylon. He was a member of the Situationist Internationale (SI) between 1958 and 1960.—*Deborah Hauptmann*]

7. [Sollers coins the word *sociomaniaque* here. "Maniaque" in French means "compulsive" in contrast to the English "maniac" meaning "crazy." He also derives the neologism *sociomane* from this and models it on words referring to addiction to a substance, such as *opiomane.*—*Trans.*]

8. [Philippe Sollers and Benoît Chantre, *La Divine Comédie: Entretiens de Philippe Sollers avec Benoît Chantre* (Paris: Desclée de Brouwer, 2000). See also "Dante and the Traversal of Writing," in Philippe Sollers, *Writing and the Experience of Limits,* ed. David Hayman, trans. Philip Barnard with David Hayman (New York: Columbia University Press, 1983), 11–44.—*Trans.*]

9. [Charles Baudelaire, *Artificial Paradises: Baudelaire's Masterpiece on Hashish,* trans. Stacy Diamond (New York: Citadel Press, 1996).—*Trans.*]

10. [Charles Baudelaire, *The Flowers of Evil,* trans. Richard Howard (Boston: David R. Godine, 1982), 11.—*Trans.*]

6. Adventure of Language, Time, Body

1. Philippe Sollers, *Théorie des Exceptions* (Paris: Gallimard, 1986).

2. Guillaume Apollinaire, *Apollinaire on Art: Essays and Reviews, 1902–1918,* ed. Leroy C. Breuning, trans. Susan Suleiman (New York: Viking Press, 1972), 280.

8. Intervention/Cézanne

1. Philippe Sollers, *L'éloge de l'infini* (Paris: Gallimard, 2001).

2. [Baudelaire uses the word *habitacle,* which in French can mean a dwelling as well as a cockpit or a binnacle. Sollers goes on to discuss the various meanings of this word. I have been forced to resort to a bit of paraphrase in order to render his thoughts into English although it should be kept in mind that "habitacle" is also an English word for dwelling, albeit an obsolete one.—*Trans.*]

3. Richard Kendall, ed., *Cézanne by Himself* (London: Macdonald, 2000), 302.

4. [The French title of Proust's book is *À la recherche du temps perdu,* literally, "the quest for time lost," which explains how well it fits in the preceding discussions.—*Trans.*]

Christian de Portzamparc is an architect and urban planner based in Paris and Rio de Janeiro. He received the Pritzker Architecture Prize in 1994 and the Grand prix de l'urbanisme 2004 in France.

Philippe Sollers is a writer, critic, and founder of the journal *Tel Quel*. He is the author of many books, including *Watteau in Venice, Event,* and *Women*. He lives in Paris.

Catherine Tihanyi, a translator and anthropologist, is a research associate in the Department of Anthropology at Western Washington University.

Deborah Hauptmann is associate professor of architecture theory at Delft University of Technology, The Netherlands. Her most recent publication is *The Body in Architecture.*